HOST WITH
CONFIDENCE

HOST WITH CONFIDENCE

French Secrets for Successful Dinner Parties

Anne de Montarlot, Bahia de Montarlot

authorHOUSE®

AuthorHouse™ LLC
1663 Liberty Drive
Bloomington, IN 47403
www.authorhouse.com
Phone: 1-800-839-8640

All photos taken from Chapter 1-5 are from Marco Fazio of MJF Studio. The illustrations in chapter 6 are from Rick Anderson of www.ooko.com.

Published by AuthorHouse 05/08/2014

ISBN: 978-1-4969-0581-9 (sc)
ISBN: 978-1-4969-0512-3 (e)

Library of Congress Control Number: 2014907468

This book is printed on acid-free paper.

For our parents Francoise and Louis, who taught us, since birth, how to create an atmosphere, be organized in a very limited time, and to always have a warm attitude with all of our dinner party guests.

CONTENTS

ACKNOWLEDGMENTS

We would like to thank Marco Fazio from Mjf Studio, Esther Lajszner, Karen Weixel-Dixon, and Farrah Wase-Bailey for all of their help and expertise in putting together this book.

PREFACE

Let's face it—in the U.S. today—entertaining at home is either all or nothing. Either we go all out or we avoid the hassle altogether.

Call us crazy, but we are almost hyperventilating from our excitement to tell you that it is not a hassle, or a stressful undertaking, to cook and entertain at home for your immediate family or for invited guests! We are also here to tell you that you absolutely should start entertaining at home more often, and not limit yourself to Christmas, the odd birthday, Thanksgiving, a BBQ or a potluck.

Do you remember going to someone's house for a dinner party, and thinking about it a whole year later? We'll tell you what you won't remember. You won't remember the food. You won't remember the drinks. You won't remember the decor. You will remember the ambiance and how you felt, with its intangible characteristics. It is just like a good Kennedy, Obama or Churchill speech. You don't really remember the words, but you remember what it made you feel like. It is the same thing with a good dinner party. You want your guests (and yourself) to remember how much fun you had, how warm and humorous the room was, and how you nearly fell off your chair laughing at your friend Larry's jokes on how he shared a two hour car ride with his mother-in-law.

And that's the trick—THE AMBIANCE.

What is an ambiance? An ambiance is the atmosphere (the five senses, the company, and the connection) and mood that you co-create and share with others over a meal. It is special. An ambiance is to a dinner party what water is to a fish. It is an experience you go away with and remember.

Ambiance is what this book is all about. It is a guide on how to create an ambiance on a practical and psychological level, and how to relax while doing so. This is not a cookbook, or an etiquette book, or a French culture book, or a floral arrangement book, or a book on how to decorate. It is all of these elements put together to create that special experience. So by all means, keep your cookbooks and use them in tandem with this one.

When Francoise—Anne and Bahia's mother—moved from Paris, France and first stepped foot in the U.S. in the early 1980's, she was immersed into an American environment devoid of the gourmet shops or upscale supermarkets that are so widespread today. Her career took away much of her free time and she was frequently travelling back and forth between Paris and New York (and smuggling in plenty of cheese, *pâté, foie gras* and *saucisson sec* with her).

Francoise didn't have much time to cook at home, let alone entertain, yet she always did! She regularly invited her new American friends to the house, all of whom had a great time, and who still remember these dinner parties thirty years later. By the same token, Francoise did not have any special secret recipes or cookbooks, nor was she a particularly talented cook, but she had three tricks up her sleeves:

(1) She knew how to create an atmosphere.
(2) She knew how to organize herself even if time-squeezed.
(3) And most importantly, she always had a lot of enthusiasm.

Following suit, Anne and Bahia, both French, have lived in the U.S. for well over twenty years (Anne has been living in London for the past thirteen years, and Bahia has been in New York most of her life). This made them completely Franco-American and bi-cultural.

Having said that, one thing kept on popping up and intriguing them:

Why did Americans make home entertaining such a big deal, while the French did not?

Preparing a meal at home, for family or friends, was done for every and all occasions. From inviting your spouse's business partner over, to having a last-minute fondue with the neighbours, or eating romantically with your boyfriend. The list is endless.

Now, restaurants are a great place to taste different foods and to relax. But you don't own it because by definition, it does not come from you. It belongs to the restaurant.

So why entertain at home?

You want to connect.

It is the most direct and effective way to connect with people and feel a true *joie de vivre*. In our virtual world of emails, texting, Facebook and Twitter, we are slowly but surely drifting into a no man's land of virtual reality stripped of real intimacy and connection. In a society infused with materialism, the cost is often poorer interpersonal relationships.

Your family is important.

Even with our busy lifestyles, we can still meet in the evening for dinner, as a family. A daily family dinner creates greater communication, social cohesion, and replenishes us with doses of closeness. This, in turn, helps establish family traditions, which could be passed onto your children. Also, children, by definition, learn about basic social skills right at home. You want them to be able to show their emotions, be outgoing, polite and communicative in life. What better way then to learn these skills at the dinner table?

You don't want to gain weight.

Eating and entertaining at home teaches you, indirectly, how to eat. And that's the key to weight management. Going out is always more fattening. The surrounding might be aesthetically pleasing and the food good, but you never know what's really on your plate. Restaurants have no problem adding butter, oil, salt and bigger portions to your dish. Plus, the minute you are seated, you are served bread and butter, which are hard to resist. The dishes are, for the most part, very rich and copious. At home, you can balance the calories and the nutritional value. You know the ingredients that you are buying and how they are being used. You own it. It is time to take back control on how you are feeding yourself, and at the same time, satisfy your palate with a delicious experience.

You don't want to waste money.

In today's gloomy economy, going to a restaurant or ordering take-out is always more expensive. Entertaining at home is more economical.

You want to "pay it forward."

The more you entertain at home and have your guests enjoy themselves, the more your guests will be inclined to do the same. People will be less afraid and intimidated at the idea of inviting people into their homes and lives.

And lastly, but most importantly, because **it is FUN**.

You do not have to turn a dinner party into a small wedding by cooking everything from scratch, displaying an over the top table setting or buying an exquisite bouquet. It is not about being a perfectly perfect host in a perfectly perfect home with a perfect dinner. You can easily and joyfully create your own ambiance right at home, without turning into the *Bridezilla* version of a host or hostess.

Perfection is a veneer, guys! It doesn't exist! You don't have to make everything perfectly, because if you do, you're missing the point and missing out on a lot of fun.

Here's why the French insist on entertaining at home:

—Because the French know and understand the three main ingredients to a successful dinner party: **the ambiance, the preparation** and **the mind-set.** This is an undying truism and formula that makes the guests comfortable regardless of their social class, age or income.

—Because going out to eat, if we dare say, should be restricted to the practical work lunch or the occasional restaurant treat.

—Because the French entertain and cook at home the most out of any Western country. Mealtime is sacred and not to be taken lightly at all! In fact, there are studies that show the average length of time spent on family dinners at home. The French spend an average of one hour; the Americans twenty minutes. In France, eating together as a family or with friends equals to a greater sense of connection and fulfillment with our immediate environment. It makes us happier.

—Because it isn't—and shouldn't be—a chore. It is a way of enjoying people's company. It is a philosophy that we'd like to share with you and which is adaptable to every culture and every person.

And we have just one rule: NO PLASTIC ALLOWED. If you are gung-ho about this, then there is no need to read on.

If you're interested in learning how to entertain the French way, here's what we have for you.

This book has three parts.

The first part of the book delivers all the different ambiances that capture the richness and diversity of French culture. From Bistro, to Mon Cheri, to Marrakech up to the Mont Blanc!

The second part of the book covers all the psychological props that will help you get the right attitude completely stress-free; like how to be confident and charismatic.

The final part covers the ground rules to follow in organizing: table top setting, type of menu, as well as all atmospheric props like smell, touch, sound, sight and all around finesse.

The ambiances are easy to achieve. They are here to inspire and give you ideas. Depending on the ambiance you choose, your guests will immediately have something in common to talk about and they will know what to bring!

Bienvenue Chez Nous . . .

"After a good dinner, one can forgive anybody, even one's relatives."

Oscar Wilde

PART I

LES AMBIANCES

An ambiance is a crucial part of any successful dinner party.

An ambiance is the whole of many parts. And this whole has to be harmonious. During an intimate dinner, you are not going to put loud music on and blind your guests with bright lights. Just like with a rustic or casual dinner, for example, you are not going to place crystal glasses or silverware. Everything has to be coordinated and coherent for the right occasion. This is the reason why we incorporate in each ambiance the following elements: tablecloth, cutlery, glasses, types of dishes, flowers, music and lights.You may decide to copy them or get inspired by them, and of course, add your own personal touch to them.

The ambiance, or atmosphere, transforms and transcends your interior by giving it a special cachet. Depending on the occasion, we are proposing typical French ambiances, regularly enjoyed by French people and easy to recreate.

An ambiance fits a specific occasion—business dinners, birthdays, Valentine's day, a 50th wedding anniversary, a graduation and so on. It is a little bit like a costume party—only not as over the top. Ambiances have different shades. That is the reason why we have carefully crafted and selected a certain number of atmospheres and themes, all distinct from one another.

It is useful to specify that these ambiances are not connected to any specific location. You can choose a rustic ambiance for a city dinner party—just like you don't have to wait to be in the mountains to enjoy a Fondue *Savoyarde* with your guests.

> ➢ All of our menu suggestions can be found on Google, YouTube, or in any French cookbook. **For each starter, main dish and dessert, we offer you a selection of two or three dishes from which you can choose from.**
> ➢ For most of our dishes, the recipes take 20-30 minutes to prepare. Some can be made last minute, while others can be prepared the day before.
> ➢ For roast cooking, we suggest the slow cooking method (at low temperatures). This enables you to achieve more tender results, while also giving you plenty of time to prepare anything else (including cleaning, setting the table, etc).
> ➢ Regarding the wines: in each of our ambiances, we have listed a few wine suggestions. The reason why we chose the wines that we did, is because they are a nice match for the specific food and ambiance choices we provided. All of the wines are from France—however—you are free to pick wines from anywhere in the world.

CHAPTER 1

Casual Ambiances

The aim of a casual ambiance is to make your guests feel cosy and comfortable, as if they were at their home . . . but with a twist! You will immerse them into a typical French ambiance. Think piles of plates, pots and pans, and a bit of a mess in the kitchen while everyone is still laughing in the dining room. It is all about chilling in chaotic style.

LE BISTRO AMBIANCE

Occasions

The Bistro ambiance is great for informal invitations to friends, family or neighbours. It is suited for the last minute visit of the mother-in-law and perfect for girly dinners where the husband finds refuge in the TV room. Poker night with the guys is also a good idea.

Why This Title?

The French have their bistros. The English have their pubs. Curiously enough, this word has a Russian origin, meaning "fast", and has become the most recognized word in France and throughout the world to designate a café where one can have a glass of wine. You can also enjoy an unfussy and comforting lunch served quickly by the *garçon*. Bistros populate the entire country of France, from the countryside, to midsize cities and of course in Paris' various *arrondissements*. The word has become so popular that its meaning morphed from a typical small restaurant to a recognizable and unique type of restaurant. In any home decor shop, you can ask the staff for a bistro glass and they'll know what you are talking about.

Francoise's Experience

Around lunch time on a Saturday, one of my neighbours, who we grew quite fond of, called to tell us that her son-in-law was visiting and staying over the weekend. She mentioned he was a bit of a hippy but loved France, good French wine (a bit too much to her liking) and was nostalgic about a terrace bistro where he would look at the world passing by. Seconds later, she asked me if they could stop by and say hello. We were in the middle of summer, about to start lunch. We agreed and told them to come by in an hour. On the spot we thought that creating a bistro-like setting would be fun, except we did not have a terrace, but a porch!

Running in the house, we took the *Vichy* tablecloth from the armoire, defrosted a baguette and some French fries (very thin ones, *pommes allumettes*) and rinsed a very dusty pile of white porcelain plates stored in our dining room cupboards. Our everyday wine glasses, bistro style, were clean in the dishwasher and we had already prepared a lentil salad the day before. We just went to the nearby supermarket to buy some good entrecote steaks. We did not have any tarts for dessert, only some Brie cheese. We cooled the Beaujolais wine bottles in the fridge. Bahia fetched the anemone flowers from the living room to place them in the center of the round table while Louis plugged the CD player (yes, we had CD's at that time!) in the electrical extension he found. Now everyone could hear the fabulous music of *Galliano*, the most Parisian accordion player of France.

With very little warning, we managed to be ready on time and our neighbor's son-in-law loved it! As he was leaving, he kissed me on both cheeks with watery eyes saying that in the U.S. he had never experienced such a bistro atmosphere, even when he went to French restaurants. He parted by saying, "I don't need to go to Paris any longer, thanks to my mother-in-law's neighbors!" This made us happy.

Bistro Table Setup

—*Table*: A square or rectangular table for four to six people, or a round bistro shaped table for two people like in a café. Wooden bistro chairs if available.

—*Tablecloth*: *Vichy* print in either red and white or blue and white. Vichy can also be known as gingham print.

—*Napkins*: Plain color and in cotton (gives an air of bistro chic) and always stay with the dominant colors of the tablecloth. The napkins should be folded and placed in the wine glasses.

—*Cutlery*: No formal silverware. Stainless steel or metal preferred.

—*Glasses*: Balloon wine glasses in plain glass (they are not expensive and you can find them from a wide price range).

—*Plates*: Hotel porcelain plates in plain white, or white with colored edges (navy blue or red are always good).

—*Butter Dish*: This is actually an indispensable signature detail for a bistro. One round dish in sandstone filled up with butter, or any nice butter display works.

—*Serving Dish*: Same style as the plates; in porcelain or stainless steel.

—*Salad Bowl*: Same as the plates in white porcelain.

—*Salt and Pepper Set*: Dark wood in standard size or a tall pepper grinder.

—*Bread basket*: Tin or wicker with a white paper napkin at the bottom. Serve a freshly-cut baguette 30 minutes before the meal. Do not warm it up! In the absence of a baguette, you can substitute it with any round country bread.

—*Carafe*: Sandstone or glass in clear or dark green. You can put the water in the carafe.

—*Wine Bottles*: We recommend that you place the wine bottles on the table, rather than in a carafe.

Bistro Décor

—*Flowers*: Seasonal and chosen for their simplicity. Very fresh and unassuming anemones are best. Better to avoid roses and lilies since this is a casual ambiance.

—*Music*: For a French bistro ambiance, nothing is better than an accordion tune.

Download songs by French artists like Galliano, Yves Montand, Jacques Brel and Charles Aznavour. Songs like *Les Feuilles Mortes, La Vie en Rose* and *C'est Si Bon* bring an air of *bal musette* to people's minds.

—*Scent and Candles*: Havana and leather candles placed around the room—not on the dining room table.

—*Extra Touch*: The host can also wear an apron, especially if it is one from the early 1900s, or in plain navy blue or black like a true *garçon* de café!

Bistro *Apéritif*

You can prepare this a few minutes in advance in the kitchen.

—*The Drinks* : A Kir is white Burgundy wine mixed with a little fruit crème liquor *(like crème de cassis)* served in bistro balloon wine glasses. The Kir is very popular inside and outside of France. It is the perfect drink for a bistro setting. It was created, like so many famous beverages and cocktails in France by a monk, in the region of Dijon. The city of Dijon is located in the heart of Burgundy, equally famous for its mustard and for being the birthplace of the Kir. The monk had the idea of adding crème de cassis with the delicious white Burgundy. Since then, the fruit cream liquor has expanded. You can use apricot, raspberry, fig, violet, etc., as well as other non dry white wines such as a Muscadet or Chardonnay. Always serve very cold white wine.

—Non-alcoholic beverages: Tomato juice with celery salt; Perrier with a slice of lemon; or other soft drinks.

—*Serving Tray*: Retro advertising tray or anything vintage-looking.

—*Aperitif nibbles*: Peanuts, *saucisson sec* (or salami cut into thin slices), and a handful of small red radishes.

Bistro Menu

Everyone is sitting down at the table and is served by the host, or the various dishes are passed from one person to the next.

Starter:

—Mash lettuce crowned with cube diced beetroot or boiled and crumbled eggs, topped with a vinaigrette dressing.

—Lentil salad with shallots and parsley, mixed with a vinaigrette dressing.

—Steamed leeks covered with a line of vinaigrette dressing.

—Six escargots of Burgundy. You will need to buy the escargots cooking platter and the escargots. Once you have purchased this, you simply put the escargots in the platter, place it in the oven, and eat with an open mind. Be sure to have plenty of bread to taste the amazing butter-garlic-parsley sauce.

Main dish:

—Steak tartar with very thin French fries.

—Entrecote (sirloin cut steak) served with very thin French fries.

—Calf liver with mashed potatoes.

Fish:

—*Meuniere*-style sole filet (grilled in melted butter) with boiled baby potatoes. You can add Hollandaise sauce as an added option too.

—*Moules Mariniere*s (cooked mussels) with very thin French fries.

Dessert:

—An assortment of cheeses such as *Camembert, Brie* or *St. Marcellin.*

—A very thin apple tart with a scoop of vanilla ice cream on top.

Wine:

—For red wine, there are widespread and affordable wines such as those from *Languedoc-Roussillon,* or other light wines from different regions such as a Pinot Noir (Alsace region), and a Chinon (Loire region). These wines are a perfect and palatable match for the rustic Bistro ambiance. If you prefer stronger and more raw blends of reds, there is always the *Beaujolais* Village or a good *Cahors.*

—For white wine, a dry Muscadet (Loire region) can easily accompany a fish dish or *moules-frites* (steamed mussels). The same goes for a Sancerre (Loire region). If you prefer a fruitier wine, the selection is large and ranges from a Sylvaner (Alsace region), to a l'Entre Deux Mer (Bordeaux region), or a Chablis (Bourgogne region).

Coffee:

The espresso is served in an espresso cup matching the plates, in white porcelain. A separate small milk pot is on the side (although in France we only add milk for morning coffee, as it is harder on the digestive process after a real meal). We recommend raw cane sugar such as the brand *Les Perruches.*

NORMANDIE AMBIANCE

Occasions

The Normandie ambiance is lovely for casual receptions of family gatherings such as a Sunday lunch or dinner. It is recommended when children are invited. This ambiance is perfect for close friends and friendly neighbours who are coming for brunch.

Why This Title?

About a century ago, the majority of French people still lived in small cities or farms and were referred to as people from *La Province* by the Parisians (anyone living outside of Paris). Agriculture was dominant in the economy. And just like with most other western countries, there was a major shift to urbanization, where mega-cities redesigned the face of France. This in turn changed people's relationship with food—how to buy it, and how to prepare it.

Despite the urban development that is so widespread today, most city slickers are still harboring a nostalgia for the countryside, which is still a very rich and varied side of France. The famous cycling race called the *Tour de France* carries riders throughout all the French countryside, zig-zagging through the hills, valleys and forests. Also, many French people make a point at having a weekend country place for which they religiously brave the Friday night traffic.

The uniqueness of France exists because of its rich variety in landscape (including two large mountain ranges, three seas and multiples prairies). Although France is not a very large country (580 miles from east to west; and 600 miles from north to south), the climate and topography are very varied. As a result, the food is diversified between all of the regions of the country. Each region has its own kind of meats, fish, and vegetables, and each accompanied with the specific wine, cheese, and dessert of the land, or *terroir.*

For well-off Parisians, the north-western coast containing Normandie has become the symbol of a return to that authentic feeling. Think of a log fire under wooden beams—the rustic elegance of houses covered with stack hay roofs—the revitalizing surrounding nature, with its fields of apple trees and, of course, its many cheeses including the famous *Camembert* cheese. Whether you cast an eye on the Normandie seaside, forest or prairie, the same realness comes across. The Normandie ambiance, very different from the city Bistro ambiance, is easy to set up thanks to the rustic but delicious dishes we are about to describe.

Anne's Experience

I remember moments or phases where just the thought of coming up with what we were going to eat for dinner infuriated me. Not only did I perceive the dinner chore as 100% my responsibility (even though I had a supportive partner), the idea of dragging myself to the supermarket aisles, uninspired and tired after a long day's work made me cringe right down to my stomach.

On the other hand, buying takeout to microwave was equally uninspiring! So, where to begin? Meat? Fish? Quiche? French? Italian? Chinese? Lost in my thoughts in the bus, I called a friend to vent, which she was all too familiar with. Her suggestion? Why not do a little picnic at home, on my rug and in front of a good film. But "make something good" on that rug, she warned!

I loved the idea, so I opted for a typical countryside menu served on two wooden boards, one with *charcuterie* and cold meats and the other with cheeses. From my 32nd floor flat, I enjoyed for an evening what people back home did on weekends. It felt strangely reassuring. It seemed easy and accessible, nothing to prepare or warm up. I had a set of stoneware plates. I emptied an old picnic wicker basket full of old hats and filled it up with four different breads. My partner, excited by this impromptu change, chilled some red wine and was about to insert the DVD in the player when our neighbor rang to ask if he could borrow our corkscrew. Puzzled by what he saw, the tablecloth on the floor with all the goodies on it, he started to blush and excused himself for bothering us as we were obviously celebrating an intimate occasion. Laughing, we invited him to join us to share our small rustic feast.

Normandie Table Setup

—*Table*: A round or rectangular table. All the dishes are spread out on the table before any guests arrive.

—*Tablecloth*: Rustic in thick cotton or rough linen with a vivid plain color or a flowery print. A patchwork tablecloth also has a nice flair to it. An added grain sack runner adds a rustic touch.

—*Napkins*: Rough linen look that can match with the color of the tablecloth.

—*Cutlery*: Simple and rustic in wood or colored stainless steel. You can place all of them in a rustic pitcher and place it on the table.

—*Glasses*: Large tumblers.

—*Plates*: Faience, stoneware or any antique looking plates. This is the only ambiance where you can mix and match your plates.

—*Butter Dish*: Round stoneware.

—*Serving Dish*: Large wood cutting boards. Rustic or antique dishes or trays.

—*Salad Bowl*: Wood or vintage.

—*Salt and Pepper Set*: A tall pepper grinder in wood. A selection of gourmet salts such as *sel de guerandes* or any local rough rock salt adds a nice touch too.

—*Bread basket*: Rattan or wicker. You can also use different types of breads placed in an antique looking granny *soupiere* tureen.

—*Carafe*: Thick glass clear or tinted. Retro porcelain or glass with a "grandma" feel to it.

—*Wine Bottles*: Wine bottles on the table getting chilled in a large bucket full of ice for both reds and whites.

Tip: Do not forget to add Dijon mustard with all the meats. Never use mustards that appear very yellow in color or too sweet in taste. You can put the mustard and other condiments all in the middle of a "lazy suzy" or just as it is. A large French pickle pot is also recommended (and by "pickle" we mean the small and crunchy ones referred to as *cornichons*).

Normandie Décor

—*Flowers*: Fresh-cut flowers like wildflowers, daisies, poppies, or lilacs placed in a glass jar. You may also substitute the flowers for a fruit bowl or a large plate made of pewter and full of apples.

—*Music*: Jazz from Michel Jonasz songs like *La Boite de Jazz and Joueur de Blues*.

—*Scent and Candles*: Wooden rustic candelabra or a large round candle as a centerpiece.Or small round candles dispersed on the table. Scents such as fresh cut grass, lilac, verbena or sandalwood.

Tip: To add to the atmosphere, if you have a spare pan or several cooking objects in old copper, do not hesitate to place them on the dining room table. Parisians love to add a touch of genuine old-fashioned objects. They represent the testament to an old home-cooking tradition. You can display them alone or put flowers, a few wisps of straw or a small stack of wheat in it.

Normandie *Apéritif*

You can prepare this a few minutes in advance in the kitchen.

—*The Drinks*: Cold white wines or chilled young reds. Apple cider (alcoholic or non-alcoholic)

—Non-alcoholic drinks like virgin Bloody Mary's.

—*Serving Tray*: Anything rustic looking in wood.

—*Aperitif nibbles*: Fresh small radishes, cut slices of salami and hard cheeses, carrots and celery sticks sprinkled with lemon, sea salt and olive oil.

Normandie Menu

Everything lies in the presentation of the food. It is important to convey the rustic touch by displaying the food on various dishes. Place a large pot of mustard, such as *Grey Poupon*, as well as French pickles, in a sandstone pot. Include two or three bread baskets and an old-fashioned tureen full of fruits or vegetables. Don't hesitate to buy a big artisan block of butter that you will display on a rustic plate. It looks very decorative.

Starter:

—One tray with a selection of *charcuterie* served on a bed of salad including *pâtes*, salamis, and smoked ham, such as *Bayonne* ham.

—One bowl of salad served as a side.

—*Chicoree* salad and garlic.

—*Campagnarde* salad including *emmental* cheese, bacon, boiled potatoes, boiled eggs and croutons.

—Any fresh salad where you add blue cheese, apples or pears, walnuts and ham.

Main Dish:

—Organic grilled chicken with chopped garlic served with roasted vegetables. You can also slow cook it at a low temperature for a few hours, which will diffuse a delicious aroma in the room.

—Mushroom or chive omelet.

—*Pot au Feu* (cooked the day before) served with a salad.

—*Bœuf Bourguignon* (cooked the day before) served with salad.

Cheese:

—*Reblochon, Comte* or a large wheel of *Brie* served on a decorative wine leaf or straw bed.

—Baked *Camembert* with rosemary.

Dessert :

—Cherry *Clafoutis*

—Fruit crumble

Wine :

Since most of the food choices contain meat, you may want to choose a soft red wine like the Bourgueil (Loire region), or a Saint Emilion (Bordeaux region), or a Cote de Beaune (Bourgogne region).

Coffee: Espresso

LA PROVENCE AMBIANCE

Occasions

Friends gathering, family gathering, and some business clients you're comfortable with can be invited to share this ambiance. We recommend it for vegetarians.

Why this title?

To the world, this region symbolizes the most relaxed and sunny area of a countryside already known for its lifestyle quality and the gusto of its food. Its sun-drenched lavender fields cover the landscape which have forever immortalized artists like Cezanne, Picasso, Van Gogh or Matisse. The abundance and diversity of its fresh local fruits and vegetables is a real treat for worldwide vegetarians and others alike. The ancestral presence of its millions of olive trees allows for an abundance of the healthiest seasoning: olive oil. The richness of its aromatic plants such as thyme and oregano transform any simple dish into a feast of *senteurs*. If you are a wine *afficionado*, you're in for a treat because *Provencal* vineyards produces *Côtes du Rhone* and the licorish liquor *Pastis* that one can drink for the *apéritif*. The *Provence* ambiance enables us to welcome a variety of guests, all different but unified in sharing the extraordinary combination of colors, scents and gastronomy.

Francoise's Experience

During the summer, I enjoyed inviting some of my American clients and Indian suppliers over. Often, as we were finishing lunch, and once we were past some of the business conversations, they wondered and asked me if it was a daily custom for us to eat like that. What they meant was whether I would put a nice tablecloth, place the plates and glasses in coordination with the color of the table cloth, and create a nice atmosphere on the table—which in their eyes—looked like a bit of an effort.

I had to be honest and confessed to them that although it was a daily practice, it was also a big source of fulfillment to me. Nothing was really a stretch or a secret when it came down to preparing a simple and colorful table. The fresh flowers laced with the freshness of the ingredients were the winning treasures. My Indian suppliers loved the fact that they could mix local vegetarian dishes with a fruity *Côtes du Rhone* wine or even some *Pastis*, all of which made them very enthusiastic! It is safe to say that both the American clients and the Indian suppliers were happy to come year after a year to Provence.

La Provence Table Setup

—*Table*: Any table will do.

—*Tablecloth*: Sunny vivid colors—if possible with a *Provencal* print (*soleiado*).

—*Napkins*: Plain or matching. You can place them in the middle of the plate with a raffia knot and a lavender twig on it.

—*Cutlery*: Anything but silverware.

—*Glasses*: What you usually have at home. Colored glasses can be fun for the late *Provencal* lunches.

—*Plates*: Plain yellow, red or orange porcelain.

—*Butter Dish*: Rustic like sandstone, or a small colored plate that matches the rest of the plates.

—*Serving Dish*: The same porcelain color of the plates or in wood.

—*Salad Bowl*: In wood, preferably an olive tree wood.

—*Salt and Pepper Set*: In wood or bright colors like yellow or red.

—*Bread basket*: A large wicker basket with an assortment of breads such as *fougasse*, a country bread with walnuts and olives.

—*Carafe:* Porcelain or sandstone.

—*Wine Bottles*: On the table in a large wine cooler full of ice to chill the whites and the famous *Provencal* Rosé.

—*Extra touch*: Any glass olive oil and balsamic vinegar bottles (not from the supermarket) are a nice display for your table decor. Choose a good looking set. Alternatively, if you happen to have a gourmet extra virgin cold presser of olive oil, keep the bottle on the table. Like a great wine bottle, these authentic attributes deserve to be seen and their provenance displayed.

La Provence Décor

—*Flowers*: Lavender, in a pot or dispensed on the table or lavender of the sea in a vase. Sunflowers are also typically *Provencal* (think Van Gogh). A couple of basil and thyme small decorative pots are useful in the kitchen and also decorative on the table.

—*Music*: Any type of sunny melody like Brazilian music, Claude Nougaro: *Dansez Sur Moi,* and Nino Ferrer: *Le Sud.*

—*Candles and Scent:* Fig, lavender or mimosa.

La Provence *Apéritif*

—*The Drink*: *Pastis* with lots of water and ice cubes. Very chilled rosé wine. Another regional specialty is to pour a drop of blueberry liqueur in a glass of very chilled rosé wine. It is called a *Myro.*

—*Serving Tray*: A wood or rustic looking one, covered with bright-colored, large napkins.

—*Aperitif nibbles*: Olive paste on toasts called *tapenade*, (from either green or black olives).

A bowl of black wrinkly olives sprinkled with *herbes de Provence.*

La Provence Menu

Starter:

—A large *Panier* of *Crudites,* which is a whole wicker basket full of raw vegetables displayed in a *pele mele* style (mix and match). This includes different types of tomatoes, peppers, radishes, cucumbers, a bunch of baby violet artichokes. You can serve it with a thick mustard vinaigrette or an *aioli.*

—*Salade Nicoise.*

—Thin onion tart, *Pissaladiere* (can be baked the day before).

—Baked *Provencal* tomatoes filled with garlic butter and parsley.

—Melon slices with *Bayonne* ham.

Main dish:

—Small Lamb chops seasoned with *herbes de Provence*, served with *ratatouille* (can be cooked the day before). New Zealand lamb chops are very good and easily available.

—*Provencal tarte tatin,* a salty, delicious version of the traditional sweet *tarte tatin* combining all the *Provencal* vegetables.

—Fish: Sea bass cooked in sea salt called *loup de mer au gros sel,* served with *ratatouille.*

This is one of the easiest fish dishes to make. Get a large piece of sea bass, leave the skin on, then smatter it with an entire box of the thickest sea salt you can find and place it in the oven. Serve with roasted vegetables (zucchini, red onions, peppers, small potatoes and large garlic chunks covered with rosemary, salt and olive oil).

Cheese:

A mix of different goat cheeses. There are various shapes available, from round to pyramidal to briquette style. Some are freshly made and soft, others more mature and hard. You can place them on a wooden board, on a bed of wine leaves.

Dessert:

An apricot tart, as it symbolizes the *Rhone* Valley.

Wine:

The *Provence* region of France happens to be particularly blessed by mother nature as it produces all of the wines: reds, whites and rosés—all of which match the foods and flavours of the region. Depending on your budget, you have the choice ranging from a red *Ventoux* to a *Cotes du Rhone* (Gigondas, Chateauneuf du Pape), or a white St. Joseph, or a Coteaux d'Aix rosé.

Coffee:

Espresso, herbal tea, mint tea or verbena tea.

MARRAKECH AMBIANCE

Occasions

This is the exotic ambiance that makes you want to travel! Great for family and close friends. We chose to unleash a Morrocan theme, but you can apply any exotic or ethnic theme too. You can apply it to an Indian, Thai, or Ethiopian ambiance as well.

Why This Title?

The restaurants where one can eat a couscous dish are growing in numbers throughout France. This exotic dish has become a staple of French gastronomy. Whether you can enjoy it at a basic *estanco* restaurant or at a more refined one, you will always keep with the French and North-African tradition. Therefore, French people don't have to travel to Morocco, Tunisia or Algeria to enjoy a real couscous. You can bring North Africa right to your dining room and go ethnically wild!

If you ask any Parisian about a couscous, what naturally comes to mind is the *quartier* of *Barbès*. Located at the bottom of the *Montmartre* hill in Paris, it is the epicenter of the North African atmosphere and is quite "soukish" in its look—vibrant with many different shops selling spices, fabric, and artisan objects. The neighborhood is inhabited by diverse communities of immigrants.

For people who don't know each other well, this type of setup is the perfect interactive food, along with *Mont Blanc, Les Grillades*, the casual *Buffet Maison* and the *Mini Din-Din* ambiances. That is because everyone participates and passes around the plates in a relaxed way. This ambiance is one that brings an air of exoticism and yet is also very French. The concept, whether from different regions of France, or from different countries of the world, holds the idea of having one main dish that is shared by everyone. In France, we tend to explore various cultures, such as with the ambiance *Chandeleur* with its crêpes, or *Alsacienne* with a big plate of *Choucroute,* or from the South West country proud of its big *Cassoulet* dish. The point is to add an ethnic or exotic theme to your ambiance, allowing you to travel without actually leaving your home.

Anne's Experience

Following a trek in the Atlas Mountains of Morocco, a friend of mine brought me some beautiful *Berber* pots. Two broke while moving but the main *tagine* pot survived and each time, it operated magically. Quite an imposing object by its size, its colors and an unevenness that marks the tradition of a *Berber* artisan, it always took a bit of ownership of the event and commanded respect. I was and still am amazed by the evocative power of an object and the attachment I have developed towards this one in particular. It brings to mind a multitude of souvenirs like magic dust invading the room. At this kind of dinner party, the pot was placed in the center of the table, surrounded by many smaller dishes following the traditional oriental dinner party. It elevated the whole table and brought an exquisite touch of exotica. Once the *cloche* was lifted, a boiling hot *tagine* appeared in front of our eyes, letting the succulent scent invade the room, and inviting all kinds of commentary and questions. Magic was there.

Marrakech Table Setup

—*Table*: A low table is the best with everyone sitting around on big cushions.

—*Tablecloth*: A white tablecloth with a gold rim or gold motif. It has to look oriental, full of embroideries and gold. In the winter, you can use any deep red velvet with gold powder sprinkled on it.

—*Napkins*: Plain in rich, thick cotton.

—*Cutlery:* Anything casual. Soup spoons are necessary.

—*Glasses*: Typical Moroccan colored glasses (especially the small tea glasses).

—*Plates*: Large soup plates to receive the bouillon of the dish alongside the meat and the vegetables.

—*Serving Dish*: The one and only *tagine* pot. It's elegant and exotic top renders a special touch difficult to match in other casual ambiances. You can buy them almost anywhere.

—*Carafe*: A glass carafe with a touch of rose water.

—*Wine Bottles*: Set on the table.

Marrakech Décor

—*Flowers*: Flowers that have a strong perfume such as jasmine or jacinth. You may also throw some rose petals on the tablecloth.

—*Music*: Middle East compilations, or worldly music mixes like *Buddha Bar* or *Cafe del Mar*. The *Gypsy Kings* work great for this theme too.

—*Scents and Candles*: Small candles with orange, jasmine, musk or patchouli aromas.

Marrakech *Apéritif*

You can prepare this a few minutes in advance in the kitchen.

—*The Drinks*: Any liquorice based drink, such as the French *Pastis* or the Greek *Ouzo*. You mix it with plenty of water and ice in each glass.

—Non-Alcoholic Drink: Squeeze lemon with a bit of sugar served with ice and a mint leaf.

—*Serving Tray*: Copper, bronze, or silver tray.

—*Aperitif nibbles*: Pistachios, black olives and grilled *merguez* sausages.

Marrakech Menu

Main dish:

—Couscous: *The Couscous Royal* carries the most with the meat, the vegetables and the bouillon. You can do it with lamb or chicken. The semolina is served on the side from another dish. The *harissa* sauce is typical as well, but be aware as it is extremely hot!

—Tagine: Many variations exists such as chicken with lemon, lamb with prunes or apricots, etc.

—Pastilla: This is a traditional Arabic dish, an elaborate meat pie traditionally made of pigeons. As pigeons are hard to get, shredded chicken is more often used today.

Dessert:

Oriental *loukoums or baklava* pastries. A nice orange fruit salad served with a plate of dates is a nice refresher and easily made.

Wine:

Here we could recommend some North African red wines such as the *Mascara* (from Algeria), or a *Boulaouane* (from Morocco). If these wines are hard to find at your local store, a rosé from *Provence* will do just fine too.

Coffee and Tea:

Jasmine tea, "white coffee" is suggested (orange flower and hot water), or Turkish coffee.

MONT BLANC AMBIANCE

Occasions

This is great for family and friends, especially over the weekend and in the winter months. This ambiance is very interactive and facilitates a sense of conviviality among the guests.

Why This Title?

The French enjoy an array of mountains: In the northeast of France are the Vosges mountains. To the east are the beautiful Alps, and in the southwest are the Pyrénées. As we mentioned earlier, the *Tour de France* cyclists do know how hard it is on their calves!

Every year during the wintertime, a large majority of French people rush to the slopes of the many ski resorts spread along the Alps. But one mountain is renowned throughout the world and that is the *Mont Blanc*, setting atop the rest of the European mountains and around which most of the resorts are located.

At night, after spending the whole day skiing, nothing is more comforting than getting together and sharing a cheese *fondue* together. In a fun, playful atmosphere, this one dish is a true winner and an attraction for everyone around. Any dull evening will be jazzed up as you place a fondue set on the table. And it's also really easy to make.

Anne's Experience

When the cold weather drags and lingers, my spirit may take a nose-dive into gloomy-town and the best remedy remains an ample dose of comfort food to share with friends. A fondue is the perfect combination of cheese, white wine and company. It seems to always work. This comes after years of going through New York's blazing snowstorms threatening to take one hostage indoors for a couple of days.

As a Parisian, I wasn't used to the extreme announcements professed by the weather channel. At first, I took each announcement very seriously, believing the end was near, and rushed after work to the supermarket to load my shopping cart with a ton of food. Later on, having survived quite comfortably through each snow storm, I changed my style and decided to celebrate it by throwing the *Soiree Savoyarde*. I was going to fight the intruder my way, from my kitchen, surrounded by friends, and sitting around a pot of fondue.

Mont Blanc—Setting the Stage

Any kind of chalet or mountain motif works here for the decor. Little print embroideries on napkins, such as snowflakes and pine trees are perfect. You can toss a knitted winter throw on the side of your sofa, add some wintery, alpine-like cushions, and voilà.

But the most important detail here is the fondue set—which should be vividly displayed at the center of the table. It is your starting place. You can add any other alpine objects or accessories. If you don't have anything off hand, place some pine branches in the middle of the table around the fondue set and some pine cones around the table. Add some red candles and you're good to go.

Mont Blanc Table Setup

—*Table*: Any size will work.

—*Tablecloth:* A thick rugged one. The colors are red and white. Use either a red plain tablecloth or a colored one like a gingham print. You can also get a printed one with winter motifs like pine trees, deer or mountains.

—*Napkins:* Match them to the tablecloth you have chosen. Cotton napkins give a much warmer and cosy feel than paper napkins.

—*Cutlery:* A fondue set cutlery (those tall, long-stem forks that you hook your bread to). Rustic cutlery for the salad and the dessert.

—*Glasses:* Plain wine glasses.

—*Plates:* In ceramic, sandstone or slate.

—*Butter Dish:* In sandstone.

—*Extra Touch:* A wooden or slate chopping board where you place the *cornichons* (small French pickles) and the *viande des grisons (bunderfleich).*

—*Salad Bowl:* Any rugged uneven wooden bowl.

—*Salt and Pepper Set:* In wood.

—*Bread basket:* In wicker or wood.

—*Carafe:* In sandstone.

—*Wine Bottles:* On the table.

Mont Blanc Décor

—*Flowers:* Any rough cuts of small decorative bramble or brushwood in a vase and pine nuts dispersed on the table. If you have any ornaments such as deer antlers or deer figurines, place them as a centerpiece.

—*Music:* Any Swiss or Austrian folkloric tunes. Light jazz like Nina Simone, *Flower* by Mission Bell—Amos Lee, *Je N'aurais Pas le Temps"* by Michel Fugain, "*Me and Mrs. Jones*" by Billy Paul, "*Melody*" by Molly Johnson, "*One of These Things First*" by Nick Drake.

—*Scent and Candles*: Pine, cedar, amber or sandalwood. You can place at the center of the table a large round candle dispensing the scent of any pine, cedar, musk, or amber.

Mont Blanc *Apéritif*

—*The Drink*: The *apéritif* is a glass of dry white wine from *Savoie*. You will continue with the same wine throughout the dinner party. Keep it light, simply because the fondue is quite a heavy meal.

Another popular *apéritif,* which one drinks at lunch or after a day of skiing is *le vin-chaud,* which literally means "hot wine"; red wine mixed with sugar, orange peels, and a bit of cinnamon. (Williams-Sonoma and Crate & Barrel usually sell these great hot wine mixes around the holidays.)

—*Aperitif nibbles*: Traditionally there is not much offered simply because the meal itself is quite filling, and one wants to keep his/her appetite intact.

Mont Blanc Menu

Starter:

This is the easiest menu possible: no starters, no sides and no preparation the day before. Everything happens around the cheese fondue pot slowly melting the cheese above a gas heater.

Main dish:

The baguette bread is cut into small pieces about 30 minutes before eating and the cheese fondue is bought all prepared. On one side of your plate will rest the special long fondue stick at the end of which you will place your bread and dip it in the fuming pot. We have a tradition in France when eating fondue. The whole game is for the guests not to have their piece of bread falling in the pot, otherwise they have to forfeit and pay the penalty of kissing the person sitting next to them! Only possible sides (on a wooden board) are some slices of *viandes des grisons, Bunderfleich,* or any mountain smoked ham like the *Bayonne* ham.

To refresh your palate, a small side plate can be added for a simple green salad.

Dessert:

Lemon or lime sorbet with a drop of vodka on top and fresh mint.

Wine:

A cheese fondue should be accompanied with dry white wine. You can choose between a Sylvaner (Alsace region), or a Sancerre (Loire region), or a Cotes de Beaune Blanc (Bourgogne region). And a Crepy (Savoie region) would add a touch of regional perfection if you can find one!

Tip: If you have problems digesting the fondue, the tradition is to have a small bit of Kirsch liquor, but be careful as it is very strong!

No coffee is needed. After eating a fondue for dinner, you will likely sleep very well!

CHAPTER 2

Formal Ambiances

Formal ambiances envelop the room with a voluptuous atmosphere where everything is about the detail.

LE QUAI D'ORSAY AMBIANCE

Occasions

You are hosting a dinner with clients or your superiors at work. Or maybe with your in-laws.

Why This Title?

Situated right next to this infamous Parisian museum (that was originally an old and beautiful train station), and located on Paris' *Rive Gauche* (the left bank of the Seine river), the *Quai d'Orsay* is one of the city's most elegant areas. It is France's symbolic headquarters for French diplomacy and style. It is an area that symbolizes the most elegance and formality of the French and how they present themselves.

The ambiance of the *Quai d'Orsay* is therefore quite formal, even if it is hosted at home. Being spontaneous in this environment is not an option. You must be a little more prepared than with the other ambiances we list in this book. For example, discretely ask your guests what they like to eat or if they have any food allergies beforehand. If the dinner is a work dinner, then the meal should be on the light side. If it is a more intimate setting among friends, then the meal should be slightly richer.

The general look is either contemporary or more antique, and in both cases, exudes sophistication.

Francoise's Experience

I had invited, many years ago, one of my largest suppliers and my most important customers at the time. I work in import/export in home decoration. My Indian supplier was already staying in my home for the past two days—which had taken a lot of my energy already in having a houseguest. We were both working all day, so there was little time for me to organize the dinner table and plan the meal. The dinner was at 7pm, and there was my supplier, my buyer, her assistant, my husband and me.

Luckily, I had thought of a little something the night before. I set the table before heading out to work in the morning by taking out a beautiful but simple table cloth that the supplier had given me as a gift (he was flattered to have his product displayed on the table, a subtle but important touch I felt). I used crystal glasses and *Limoges* plates (named after a town in France where these porcelain white plates with delicate decoration were first made). The silverware was actually made of silver. I placed a crystal vase with fresh cut flowers and I put aside a *Vivaldi* CD for some ambiance music.

Everyone came over at 7pm and I served them a *Kir Royal* as an *apéritif* (Champagne mixed in with a little *crème de cassis*) to relax a bit before dinner. The appetizer was a romaine salad with pears, walnuts and a sprinkle of blue cheese, which I first served to the buyer, then to her assistant, then to the supplier and then to my husband (the order is important).

The main course was a Long Island duck with turnips (our house was on Long Island), followed by a plate of cheese (brie, goat cheese, and *Roquefort*). The wine, which was the same wine throughout the entire dinner, was a good Bordeaux *Lalande Pomerol* (it is always a good idea not to mix the wines, and especially avoid changing from red to white or vice versa). For dessert, I took out my nice crystal champagne coupes (different from champagne flutes) and put two scoops of raspberry sorbet mixed with various berries and a pinch of *crème de cassis* liquor on the top (the same used for the *Kir Royal*). After feeling the refreshment that only a little sorbet can bring, we went back to the living room to sip a little decaf espresso with fine chocolates.

The dinner was an incredible success and the buyer (an American business woman) didn't understand how I could put together such an elegant, tasty and complete meal in such a little amount of time. She still reminds me of this dinner now, twenty years later! But this dinner was not a big difficulty. The "mystery" behind it is quite simple:

- The dishes were simple and quick to prepare. How hard is it to mix salad with walnuts and fresh ripe pears, or put a few scoops of sorbet into a glass, and unwrap the three cheeses to serve on a dish? Even though the meal was simple, the ingredients were of top quality, guaranteeing good flavor. Because it was well presented, it appeared grander than it actually was.
- The duck and turnips were cooked the night before, and warmed up one hour before serving.
- The table setting was put together in the morning, so I was able to work the whole day stress-free.
- The champagne, wine and food were bought three days prior to the dinner.

For the duration of the whole dinner party, I was only briefly absent from my guests. They thought I did not work that day at the office, but actually I was just a little organized the night before. The best part about it was that the dinner itself helped me to relax and have an enticing dinner with guests. It could have been the opposite. I could have been stressed all day from work, then gotten an adrenaline rush from preparing dinner quickly, and then being nervous because this was a work dinner. Instead, it was a delight for all of us and I didn't overwork myself or have to pay double if not three times more, had I chosen to take them out to a restaurant.

Le Quai D'Orsay Table Setup

—*Table*: Any shape will do.

—*Tablecloth*: White in a beautiful jacquard.

—*Napkins*: White with a subtle lace or contemporary appliqué.

—*Cutlery*: Silver or plated silver. Do not forget to include fish knives, spoons for dessert and one serving cheese knife too.

—*Glasses*: Crystal if possible. Otherwise your nicest wine glasses, plus champagne flutes (for the *apéritif*). You could also use colored glasses for the water glasses if they are very good quality.

—*Plates*: Use your very best. It is the perfect time to use your wedding gifts or your best China.

—*Butter Dish*: In porcelain or sterling silver.

—*Serving Dishes*: In porcelain in line with the quality of the plates.

—*Salt and Pepper*: Silver plated.

—*Breadbasket*: In silver or equivalent.

—*Carafe*: Any nice carafe (most people have one or two carafes in their home at best, so don't worry if you don't have one). Since the wine should be a really good one, you'll only be using the carafe for the water.

—*Wine Bottles*: On the table. Don't forget to add a wine bottle coaster so as not to spill any wine on the linens.

Tip: If you happen to have the little individual knife holders (where you place your knife when not eating in order to not stain the table linens), then that is an extra touch of class.

Le Quai D'Orsay Décor

—*Flowers*: Depending on the season, either roses, gladiolus, orchids or peonies. They should be classy flowers set in a sophisticated vase. On the dining table, we suggest two or three very small square or round vases with one flower, like a rose inside it. Some vases are displayed throughout the living room also where you will be having the *apéritif*. If your guests bring flowers, place these flowers immediately in a nice vase and display where the guests can see them (not in your bedroom or bathroom, for example).

—*Music*: The music should be soft, like relaxing classical music, a piano concerto perhaps, or nice ambiance music that is discreet like Bossa Nova. If your guests are from a different culture, it might be a delicate touch to put on some tunes from their country, provided it is discreet and not too loud.

—*Scent and Candles*: You can display two big candelabras with white or red candles on the table.

Le Quai d'Orsay *Aperitif*

—*The Drink*: In this setting, the *apéritif* could be a lot of things as you want to give your guests the choice. It's not a bad idea to buy the ingredients for a semi-full bar ahead of time including: whiskey, vodka, and gin, as well as cold Schweppes, Perrier and a fruit juice plus a lemon or two. No beer should be served at this kind of dinner party. This is all in addition to the wine, Champagne and water. The easiest is to offer everyone a *Kir Royal* (usually everyone enjoys this) but if someone fancies a gin and tonic, then you will be prepared for that too.

—*Serving Tray*: Anything elegant looking; traditional or contemporary.

—*Aperitif nibbles*: Accompany your drinks with some *pâté*, quail eggs or blinis with salmon eggs (very chic).

Le Quai d'Orsay Menu

The meal should be refined, not ostentatious. You don't have to go over the top with a very sophisticated food choice or the finest wine from France. The point is to communicate to your guests a sense of pleasure in meeting at your house, without having to show that you're trying to impress them. The key is to get top notch ingredients. Buying a *Chateau Lafitte* with Russian caviar is nice, but it may be trying too hard (save that for the holidays or an engagement party or something). Remember, your guests will be more marked by the relaxed ambiance that you created than the fancy food and complex wine labels.

Starter:

—Lobster and asparagus served on a bed of mash salad with homemade mayonnaise.

—*Haricot verts extra fin* (extra thin green beans) salad with *foie gras*. Lemon and olive oil dressing.

—*Langoustines Dublin Bay* with homemade mayonnaise.

Main Dish:

—*Roti de filet* (roasted filet of beef) of the best quality with sliced roasted potatoes and lightly roasted mini vegetables.

—Rack of lamb with rosemary and mustard crust served with roasted or boiled new potatoes.

Fish:

—Sea bass served with basmati rice.

—*Coquille St Jacques*(scallops) with steamed potatoes.

Cheese:

The cheese plate should be varied with goat cheese, *camembert*, a blue cheese such as *roquefort*, and if possible a Swiss *Gruyere* or *Comte*.

Dessert:

—Raspberry or strawberry sorbet with fresh berries on top, and lightly sprinkled with a little *crème de cassis.*

—Vanilla ice cream with one mint leaf on top and macaroons (such as the ones from *Laduree)* on the side.

We recommend that sorbet or ice cream should be placed in big glasses, or very small and beautiful silver bowls.

Wine:

Preferably for the meat, you should choose a red wine that is not too heavy (particularly for those that enjoy red wine with fish). We recommend a very good *Bordeaux* like the Pomerol, Pauillac, St Julien and Margaux areas. Cote-Rotie and Hermitage are also a good choice. If the main *entrée* is fish, we recommend a fruity but dry white wine, like a *Macon* or a good White *Burgundy* or a very good *Chablis* Grand Cru.

Coffee:

Espresso or a macchiato. It is more elegant to use sugar crystal sticks.

MON CHERI AMBIANCE

Occasions

This is best for Valentine's Day, a wedding anniversary or any romantic encounter. This ambiance is by definition, only for two people.

Why This Title?

This word is used by the French to indicate a couple's intimacy. *Mon Cheri* is softly whispered in private to one another. An ambiance with this name translates perfectly to the type of intimate dinner one wants to achieve. It is either to mark the beginning of a love story that might get serious or to celebrate forty years of love and commitment.

Lights are dimmed and gentle. If you can, put as many candles as possible, which can replace any other electrical lighting altogether. Candles are always flattering for one's complexion. The music is hinted only. Classical or contemporary, it has to correspond to the guest's tastes or to the couple's shared tastes. You can use the best China, cutlery, and glasses you have.

The type of food (tasty and refined) and the music are your best allies to create the mood of a *je ne sais quoi*. It will leave an unforgettable memory for the people involved.

Anne's Experience

A smile always comes to my face as I think of my best friend who was, on that occasion, a million times gutsier and adventurous than me when it comes to the matters of the heart. In order to convey to a friend that she really liked him, she took it upon herself to throw a surprise romantic dinner at her place and invite him. She lived in a tiny studio apartment, intelligently divided into her *atelier* studio (she was a *trompe l'oeil* artist), and her living quarters. If someone would have arrived impromptu, they would have to stride over paint pots to avoid falling down on her easel full of clothes, before marking a path towards a minuscule kitchen where one would enjoy an espresso sitting on recycled stools. But for this special occasion, she managed to clear some space in her highly elaborated *bric-a-brac*.

She dressed the table with a beautiful white sheet, wrote the menu on the easel and placed a superb bunch of pink roses in the middle whose scent instantly took hold of the tiny space. In a large pot of paint, a champagne bottle was slowly getting chilled. Her heart palpitating, she waited for the bell to ring. Little did her romantic friend know what was in store for him. The minute he stepped into the studio, he was time-transported into the heart of the enchanting *Montmartre* neighborhood. An Edith Piaf song would have been the last drop. I leave to your imagination what happened once that door was shut.

Mon Cheri Table Setup

—*Table*: Any small table for two. If you only have a big table, then create an intimate corner by using the tablecloth as a divider.

—*Table Cloth*: A delicate and beautiful plain red or white in fine cotton or pressed linen.

—*Napkins*: Same fabric, in white.

—*Cutlery*: In silver or plated silver/metal.

—*Glasses*: Wine glasses in crystal, and elegant water glass goblet (can be in one color) as well as Champagne flutes, preferably in crystal.

—*Plates*: Elegant white chinaware.

—*Serving Dish*: Ornate white chinaware or colored glass or silver/ plated silver metal.

—*Salt and Pepper*: Silver plated.

—*Bread basket*: In plated silver/metal

—*Carafe*: In crystal or white glass

—*Wine*: Wine bottle is on the table, placed on a silver plated coaster.

Mon Cheri Décor

—*Flowers*: Roses are the best. There is such a vast variety of colors that the choice is yours. They will emphasize the earnestness of the intimate dinner.

—*Music*: Music is very important and will contribute along with the decor, the food and the Champagne to set the mood. Prepare the playlist in advance where you can mix some French tunes with international ones. Chill out compilations are good. But most importantly, be careful for the music or the playlist not to stop abruptly, as it might create unease. The music can vary from upbeat romantic at the *aperitif* to something more sexy and intimate during and after the meal. Charles Aznavour: *Formidable*, Gainsbourg: *Je t'aime Moi Non Plus*, Edith Piaf: *La vie en Rose*, France Gall: *Une Declaration*, Francoise Hardy: *Message Personnel*, Michel Berger: *Quelques mots d'amour*, Sade: *No Ordinary Love*.

—*Scent and Candles*: If there is one ambiance where you can splash out the candles, it is this one! Candles are the romantic prop of excellence! You can spread out mini round candle holders, as well as have one beautiful baroque looking candelabra, with glass tassels in the center. You can take it away once you start eating. Around the room place scented candles such as: roses, tuberose, jacinth, violet, as well as other decorative candelabra.

Extra Touch: The two chairs can be draped with a velvet or white sheet. Peacock feathers can be added in a vase. Also, if your house or apartment has a fireplace, this is the ideal time to make use of it!

Mon Cheri *Aperitif*

—*The Drink*: Pink Champagne is best, which you can keep throughout the dinner or switch for a white wine. You can drape the neck of the Champagne bottle if you want. *Kir Royal* which is composed of *crème de cassis* liquor and Champagne is also an alternative.

—*Serving Tray:* Plated silver covered with white linen.

—*Aperitif nibbles*: Salmon eggs on *blinis* or smoked salmon on *blinis,* with some *crème fraiche.*

Mon Cheri Menu

The meal should be very refined, which is not synonymous to heavy and copious. It is the time when you can display your gourmet attributes.

Starter:

—*Foie gras* with split figs and toasted brioche bread.

—Globe artichokes with a vinaigrette dressing or melted butter.

Main Dish:

—Slow cooked beef cooked and perfumed with Indian spices such as ginger, coriander, cumin, or cinnamon—served with cooked tomatoes, green peas, and peppers. It will melt in your mouth!

—A Filet mignon served with mushroom fricassée.

Fish:

—Grilled turbot with a hint of hollandaise sauce, and steamed new potatoes served with sour cream and chives.

—King size scallops served in their shell with lemon sauce and wild rice.

—Luxurious sea bass *brochettes* that you can eat together with your hands and dip in some savory sauce of your choice.

—A tray of raw oysters. You can serve the fresh oysters with a side of horseradish, lemon, and bread and butter.

Cheese:

No cheese—too smelly for a romantic dinner.

Dessert:

Chocolate fondant or rose macaroons.

Wine:

We strongly recommend serving pink *Champagne* throughout the duration of the entire dinner, but another romantic option is the Saint Amour red wine, which is one the lightest of the *Beaujolais* crus, often displaying spiced berry and stone-fruit characters.

RIVE GAUCHE AMBIANCE

Occasions

This is great for any friends or family members you'd like to treat in a refined yet relaxed atmosphere away from the hustle and bustle of life. You are offering them an aesthetic atmosphere where you can catch up and gossip on the latest.

Why This Title?

The three *arrondissements* bordering the Seine river in Paris (the 5th, 6th and 7th) are grouped together under the iconic name of *Rive Gauche,* which has always emblemized the literary, intellectual and sophisticated Parisian scene. Amongst the cobbled streets and old street lamps, one can stroll and discover a concentration of art galleries, publishing houses and antique dealers. The Panthéon, the Sorbonne and the French Academy are also located on the *Rive Gauche.* Prestigious cafés such as *Le Café de Flore* and *Les Deux Magots* in *Saint Germain* were a second home, in the mid twentieth century, to artists, writers and intellectuals such as Jean Paul Sartre.

This Parisian location is still today a sort of intellectual hub. Most government ministers are located there, as well as the infamous French *Grandes Ecoles* (prestigious Universities educating France's elite). To live in the *Rive Gauche* is not only a sign of wealth like other chic and bourgeois *arrondissements,* it is a sign of high social status. And it is all about style. To be from the *Rive Gauche* is to be classy and well-spoken, not flashy or *nouveau riche.*

Anne's Experience

A very good friend of mine decided to rent out a trendy gallery on West Broadway (in N.Y.) and host a dinner for eight of his colleagues. The morning of the dinner party, the gallery manager had to cancel the event because there had been a fire next door, and the building was now inaccessible for a few days while post-fire work was being done. My friend was beyond bummed and stressed. He had suddenly lost his deposit for the gallery and for the catering and didn't have enough money to take the dinner party to a restaurant. It was hence a catastrophe, and he had to find a solution quickly.

The first thing he did was call his close friends to see if the party could be moved to their apartments (as his little studio in Tribeca wouldn't do). No one could help, so my sister and I volunteered my apartment, which was simple but large enough to hold a dinner party. The three of us had only a few hours to transform the place into a chic dinner party. The only contribution he could bring over was a big, white, embroidered tablecloth from Portugal. We thought the whiteness of it was a perfect start, and so the decor and food had a white theme. Bahia brought over beautiful Indian block print napkins and some old but nice plates. I took out some nice white porcelain dishes with big *Fleurs de Lys* on them and added some white tulips in a small silver vase.

The dinner started with large sea scallops, and then we had a Chilean sea bass accompanied by basmati rice. For dessert, we had a nice little portion of lemon sorbet paired with little cookies and a *Poire William* (Pear) digestive. The whole meal was showered with Champagne and white wine. Nearly everything on the table was white! We were able with a few nice ingredients and simple tablewear to transform my apartment into an elegant gallery. Everyone had a good time and was able to creatively blend together for work and fun.

Rive Gauche Table Setup

—*Table*: A glass or marble rectangular or square table.

—*Tablecloth*: Semi-light grey in cotton.

—*Napkins*: A darker shade of grey, like a grey slate.

—*Cutlery*: Anything contemporary looking.

—*Glasses*: Champagne flutes, white wine glasses (Riedel style), and water glasses.

—*Plates:* Contemporary white plates, preferably square-shaped and in porcelain. Small rectangular plates for the side bread.

—*Butter Dish*: A white porcelain round butter dish or on a small white plate.

—*Salad Bowl*: In white porcelain.

—*Serving Dish*: White porcelain or silver plated/chrome with a contemporary edge.

—*Salt and pepper set*: Silver plated or chrome.

—*Breadbasket*: Metal or aluminium.

—*Carafe*: A glass carafe that is slim and chic, not traditional. Or if no such carafe is available, you can buy sparkling or still mineral water in glass bottles (like Evian or San Pellegrino).

—*Wine bottle* on the table.

Rive Gauche Décor

—*Flowers:* They should be pretty stylish. We suggest putting one or two square shaped metal vases with white roses, tulips or peonies.

—*Music*: *Paris Paris by* Catherine Deneuve and Malcolm Mc Laren, Enzo Enzo: *Juste quelqu'un de bien,* Claude Challe, Stephane Pompignac *Costes Compilations,* Bossa Nova *like: Acontece by* Adriana Maciel,

O Grande Amor and So Danco Samba by Antonio Carlos Jobim, *Vivo Sonhando* by Getz/Gilberti. Also: *Au Fur et a Mesure* by Tres Hombres— Quartier Libre, *Carnaval de Paris* by *Dario G, Chan Chan* by Buena Vista Social Club, *Decale* by Patrick Bruel, *Epoca by* Gotan Project, *I've seen that face before* by *Grace Jones.*

—*Scent and Candles*: Two slim design candle sticks with white candles on top. Scented candles of tuberose, rose, grapefruit or black pomegranate.

Rive Gauche *Apéritif*

—*The Drink*: Champagne or Prosecco.

—*Non-alcoholic drink*: Perrier with a lemon.

—*Serving Tray*: In chrome.

—*Aperitif nibbles*: Quail eggs with celery salt. Fennel and carrot sticks with a splash of olive oil and lemon.

Rive Gauche Menu

Starter:

—*Endive* salad with Roquefort cheese and thin *haricots verts* (extra fine string beans) served with a honey mustard dressing.

—A goat cheese salad. You melt the *crottin de chavignol* cheese (small round goat cheese) on small pieces of toasted bread, and place them on a bed of lettuce. Vinaigrette or honey mustard dressing.

—Fresh white asparagus served with a light mayonnaise.

Main dish:

—Chicken *paillard* (very thin slices of chicken, from a good butcher) accompanied with thin *haricots verts* (string beans) or braised fennel.

—*Tournedos Rossini* served with strings beans and roasted thin green asparagus.

Fish:

Cod wrapped in a *Bayonne* ham served with mash potatoes or on a bed of Puys green lentils.

Cheese:

Two or three very good and varied goat cheeses served with grapes.

Dessert:

—Lemon tart or a mixed berry fruit salad with a scoop of raspberry liquor.

—*Crème brulée* (hard to make at home so it is better to buy from a good patisserie shop).

Wine:

The wine selection should match the level of intimacy and sophistication of the food choice. *Champagne* can be served throughout the whole dinner, but you can also pour a very good *Burgundy* red, such as a "Grand Cru" *Cote de Nuit,* like Gevrey Chambertin, Chambole Musigny or Vougeot.

And just as good as the *Burgundy* choices above, are some red Grand *Bordeaux* selections, like the best of the Margaux, Pauillac, or Saint Estephe.

Coffee:

Expresso or macchiato or verbena.

CHAPTER 3

Buffet Style Ambiances

The buffet is the ultimate temptation for all the senses. Dish after dish, your eyes caress the tantalising food, and you ALWAYS end up devouring more than you can. In these moments, any form of restraint or willpower Is useless. This is precisely why we love the buffet: because it is one of the rare occasions when you can let go without guilt!

LA PETITE MAISON AMBIANCE

Occasions

Any invitation where the number of guests exceeds the number of chairs at a table. A buffet is good for any occasion—formal and casual. It is also a good idea for graduations, or any family celebrations and children's parties as well.

We are proposing two versions of buffets. The first one, *La Petite Maison,* is more casual, and can also be customized to any of our other ambiances. Alternatively, you can always up your game and throw a more sophisticated buffet reception. We called it Buffet *Le Louvre* because of its pyramidal shape.

Why This Title?

The origin and meaning of the word buffet is actually a large decorative cabinet. In most of the French countryside the buffet was, and still is, a prominent piece of furniture used not only to store your dishes, but also to showcase them. Customarily located in the dining room, they are usually filled with all sorts of ornamental plates and flowery dishes and platters. When the number of guests exceeds the capacity of the dining room table, the top of the buffet is then used as the centerpiece for arranging all the dishes. Hence, it is used as a storage unit and also as a self-service display table. That is the origin of the word buffet.

Now the term has evolved to mean a big table containing all of the food for the party (not to be confused with a BBQ style option, which we discuss in our chapter about *Grillades Le Chasseur* and *Monte Carlo*).

If you're entertaining for more than eight or ten people, it isn't a bad idea to host a buffet meal instead of a sit-down meal. The buffet is convenient indoors and outdoors, and is also a good option if you have less than eight or ten guests but live in a small space without a large dining area.

The buffet ambiance is not a minimalist occasion, but more organized chaos, where mixing dishes, drinks and people is essential. The food should be presented in a more theatrical way, displaying lots of different shaped dishes and colorful food. The presentation, however, should be organized. Place all of the dishes at once if you can, perhaps with the appetizers on the left and the main dishes on the right (cheese and dessert come after).

Food aside, you can and should also include a bouquet of flowers or a centerpiece of decoration such as a sculpture, adding some art to your buffet. The different plates, cutlery and napkins should be on the side or on a smaller, accent table. The important aspect to remember is to present your food and drinks with an organized flow and symmetry. Take a typical bookshelf as an example. On the far right and far left of the books are bookends, adding support and symmetry. The same could be applied to the presentation of a buffet: adding a bouquet of flowers on both ends of the buffet and a small statue or large candles in the middle, and displaying the food in between all of these pieces.

The main dishes should be in the center, surrounded by all of the accompanying side dishes. Once the guests have finished eating the appetizers, main dishes and sides, remove everything, clean up the crumbs, (maybe even changing the table cloth if it gets stained) and present the cheese and dessert plates with grace. For the cheese, you should have a lot of different varieties. We recommend six. They too should be well presented, using leaves, large herbs or grapes to decorate your cheese plate. Always have a variety of different breads and crackers to accompany the cheese.

The desserts should also be varied and delicate, leaving your already stuffed guests salivating for more. We recommend a fruit tart, a chocolate cake, fresh fruit, and some nice side cookies or macaroons.

Under the buffet table, you could stock the wine and water bottles, so as not to go back and forth to the kitchen for refills. Also a good idea is to open up 80% of the wine you have ahead of time, to make it easier for you and your guests (just re-cork them so they don't fall and spill). In the kitchen, keep one or two vases on hand, so you can quickly place any flowers that your guests have brought for you (just don't display them on the buffet as it might not blend with the decoration you already prepared).

Bahia's Experience

Over the years, I've been invited to a lot of different buffets in the U.S. for various occasions, whether outdoors in the summer or indoors during the colder months. Buffets are always enjoyable socially because there are usually more people that attend these than sit-down meals. The other reason why I like buffets is because you can choose who you want to mingle with and what you want to eat! At a sit down event, you don't necessarily choose who you sit next to. I look at buffets much like taking a holiday cruise. Instead of flying to one Caribbean island for vacation, you get to visit five islands in the Caribbean and get a flavor of different foods and people. Similarly, at a buffet, you are not bound by one plate or by one person sitting next to you. You are a little freer to do what you want. That said, at the last buffet lunch I went to, a lot went wrong. Here's an example of what NOT to do:

It was a Franco-American couple who invited everybody to their house for a Christmas holiday lunch. There were about fifteen guests in total, who were all scattered around the buffet table finding an insufficient amount of napkins and plates. Some of the glasses were still sitting in their original carton box under the buffet table. There were lots of appetizers and a big cheese plate but no bread basket. There was no *aperitif* time, nor a written or announced menu. There was no music either.

Everyone arrived around noon and by three in the afternoon we were starting to get pretty hungry. The guests, not knowing if the food on the buffet table was the whole meal or not, indulged in all the food they saw. Since there weren't enough plates, the hosts were busy going back and forth to the kitchen cleaning plates and glasses. They had focused their attention more on replacing the plates than enjoying their friend's company—hence defeating the purpose of having fun! Many of the guests didn't know each other and were left to awkwardly introduce themselves on their own.

Finally, around four in the afternoon, the main dishes came out, but by then, the guests were full from eating all the cheese and appetizers. The buffet, even with good food and a nice decor, was a flop. There was too much chaos and no ambiance. Here are some suggestions for a more organized and fun buffet.

La Petite Maison Décor

Regarding the disposition, you can choose between two options. Either you place your dishes and plates partly on the buffet table as well as on a side table, or in the absence of a buffet, you simply use a long dining room table.

—*Tablecloth*: You can use Kraft paper as your tablecloth, with a nice colorful runner, or an off-white vintage type of tablecloth.

—*Napkins*: There are a few options here for both paper and cotton napkins. The first is to fold the napkins into all of the wine glasses ahead of time. The second option is you can wrap the forks and knives into the napkins. If either of those is too much work, then simply stash the napkins on either end of your buffet table.

—*Cutlery*: It is simple and could be wrapped in white paper napkins, held together by string or light rope.

—*Glasses*: The water glasses could be colored. The wine glasses clear.

—*Plates*: The appetizers and main dishes should be varied in shapes and sizes. The serving plates for the cheese and desserts should be displayed on more elevated, raised or turning platters, if possible. Do not forget to add some small and medium size bowls and plates for all the side dishes.

—*Butter Dishes:* You can have several round butter dishes with the small butter knife spread over the table.

—*Other Displays*: Serving trays and salad bowls can be from contrasting materials such as wood or glass. The mustard and vinaigrette should also be displayed in a presentable way. Never just put the supermarket container for either of these condiments.

—*Salt and Pepper Set*: In wood or metal.

—*Bread Basket*: One big bread basket is essential. It can also be decorated by mixing different breads, and crackers, and breadsticks.

—*Flowers*: Any fresh flowers mixed with natural fibres such as wheat, cabbages, lavender, etc.

—*Music:* Any compilations so that you always have a background melody.

La Petite Maison *Apéritif*

All the glasses are displayed on the table already for the guests to help themselves. If formal, you will have created a space specifically for the champagne glasses. If more casual, everyone can use their first glass throughout the party.

The food nibbles will be scattered around the room on various trays. The idea here is for people to move around and have a chat with many different guests.

La Petite Maison Menu

Choose three or four various salads, using different colors. For example, a lentil salad and wild rice salad. There should also be one giant, compartmentalized salad with all the vegetables like corn, avocado, tomato, cut up Swiss cheese, asparagus and red radishes.

On all these salads, do not mix the dressing, but let your guests use the vinaigrette quantity they like. Also, it is always a good idea to surround all of your salad dishes with parsley, which adds a bit of decor to your presentation.

Some other suggestions:

- Quail Eggs
- *Petit cochon* treats, which is cold *charcuterie*, meaty little slivers of happiness. Examples are *Bayonne* ham, prosciutto, salami, *pâté*, with a bit of small *cornichons,* as a delectable accessory.
- Asparagus with *tarama* (fish roe dip)
- Quiche Lorraine
- Onion Tart
- Smoked salmon or freshly cooked (cold) salmon with small new potatoes, with homemade mayonnaise
- Cheese plate (brie, sharp cheddar, goat cheeses)
- Dessert: millefeuilles (Napoleon), fruit salad or chocolate mousse

LE LOUVRE BUFFET

Occasions

This kind of ambiance could fit any kind of celebratory occasion. It could be for family, friends, or professional contacts. If there are a lot of guests, then better have it buffet style—but a formal buffet.

Why This Title?

For any anniversary, graduation, promotion or religious holiday, for which as we say in France, *On met les petits plats dans les grands*, which literally translates to putting the small plates into the big ones. What it really means is to have a party for any or all occasions and have a good time (a very French concept, by the way!). Why not have a little party that is out of the ordinary, folks? To have a party, or in our case a dinner party, for a special occasion like this, is special because this kind of event evokes a little luxury, a sort of spunky appeal with tasteful food and a delightful décor. We called it *Le Louvre* as a little wink to the majestic glass Pyramid resting in the middle of the *Cour d'Honneur* of the *Louvre* Museum in Paris.

The formal buffet has the same spirit as the casual one, except the plates, dishes, decorative items and flowers are stepped up a notch to appear more luxurious. A good idea to turn your buffet from casual to formal is to have two or three different levels on the buffet table itself, much like a pyramid. You can use plastic storage containers, a small night stand or stacks of large coffee table books to hold up these different units. Use what you have and top them off with any matching linens you have available.

Bahia's Experience: My College Graduation

Since it took me six years to obtain a Bachelor's degree instead of four, (after numerous transfers of universities between Paris, New York and Beijing and lots of jobs and internships) we were all really excited to finally end the college years and set on for the "real world"!

My mother took care of the food and ambiance for all ten guests at her Long Island home (a mix of local friends and relatives from France). Since the weather was great, she made a big table outside on the patio. There were flowers and plants everywhere, and then when evening came, outdoor candles and multi-colored lights illuminated our celebratory garden setting. We brought the music outside (a mix of Bossa nova, Gypsy Kings, Massive Attack, etc.). Of course there was plenty of Champagne for the *apéritif* with little *hors d'oeuvres* served to everyone. The dinner was all seafood (since I love it!) with little neck clams to start with, and big crabs for everyone with *camarguais* wild rice. To top it off, you guessed it, a big cake in the shape of a graduation hat (cheesy, but necessary). Then more Champagne till the wee hours. None of this would have been possible at a restaurant for only 10 people. It wouldn't have been nearly as fun and it probably would have cost a small fortune.

Le Louvre Décor

To construct your pyramid, you could use white linen as your base tablecloth, and the accented and elevated portions could be draped with taupe, beige, brown, or grey tablecloths.

The napkins should be in white cotton, or any light solid color.

At the center of the buffet display, on the highest elevated level should be a decoration piece, like a grandiose and decadent bouquet, any elegant candle holders with white candles, or a small lemon or orange fruit tree.

The second tier level should be reserved for the wine and/or Champagne (in a chilled silver Champagne bucket) and the accompanying glasses and flutes. On each side, there could be a nice pyramid of whole fruits—either mixed or you could fill up a rectangular glass vase with lemons or green apples.

The first and base level should be reserved solely for the food.

The cutlery should be silver or stainless steel metal, wrapped in white cotton napkins, and tied together with a colorful velvet or lacy ribbon.

The bread basket should be in silver or stainless steel metal with a white or an off-white linen (so the bread doesn't touch the metal).

Extra Touch: Some of the dishes could be presented with flowers, nice leaves or rose petals.

Le Louvre *Apéritif*

Champagne or Prosecco accompanied by trays of elegant *canapés*. The *canapés* are the perfect *grignotage* (or nibblers) before the rest of the food.

Le Louvre Menu

Starters:

—Smoked salmon

—Fresh crab salad

—*Foie gras*

—Fresh vegetables, crudités, with dip (cauliflower, carrots, peppers, radishes, cherry tomatoes).

Main dishes:

—Sea bass with ginger.

—*Cote de boeuf* (rib of beef).

—*Epaule d'agneau* (shoulder of lamb).

—*Meli Melo* of vegetables (assortment of cooked veggies).

Sides:

—Mache salad (lamb salad).

—*Ratatouille*

—*Pommes anglaises* (small steamed potatoes).

Don't forget to add all the different gourmet mustards for any meat dishes.

Cheeses:

Roquefort, strong and aged goat cheese, *Reblochon* and *Camembert.*

Desserts:

—"Opera" style chocolate cake.

—A pyramid of macaroons.

—Pear sorbet with bits of pear, accompanied with cigarette cookies.

CHAPTER 4

French Barbecue Ambiance

French people love a good barbecue! Smoky flavors coupled with a happy and relaxed atmosphere come instantly to mind. The centerpiece is of course the omnipotent barbecue! Synonymous to simplicity and authenticity, it has become throughout France a template of conviviality and uncomplicated fun. Once it is warm enough, we become free of those heavy winter clothes, and have more time outside to stroll the local farmer's markets. It is hence the perfect excuse to organize a *grillades*—a word that literally translates to barbecue in French.

We are describing two types of typical *grillades*: One with Mediterranean flavors for warmer temperatures, and the other adapted to the more carnivorous palate which usually takes place in colder temperatures.

GRILLADE MONTE-CARLO AMBIANCE

Occasions

This ambiance is nice for informal gatherings with friends and family.

Why This Title?

As soon as the first rays of sun appear, French people love to transplant their cherished family home meals outside by carrying their table onto their terraces, garden lawns or backyards. It is the occasion to enjoy, stress-free, the company of friends and family in the fresh air.

Grillades Monte-Carlo Table Setup

—*Table*: A wooden table that is distressed or has a "white-washed" type of look, with a table runner in light blue, or blue with a white border stripe. In the absence of this, you can also use your normal dining room table with a tablecloth.

—*Tablecloth:* Blue and off-white or coral and off-white.

—*Napkins:* Off white or camel color, in cotton.

—*Cutlery:* Bamboo style elegant finish.

—*Glasses*: Wine glasses with clear tops and colored feet. Water goblets that can be clear but rustic looking.

—*Plates*: Place your white plate on a large under plate in blue or coral (plain or with a motif) depending on the tablecloth you have chosen.

—*Butter Dish:* In plain off white.

—*Serving Dishes:* In blue, off white or coral color.

—*Salt and Pepper Set*: In wood, off white.

—*Bread Basket:* In metal or light wood.

—*Carafe:* In clear white glass.

—*Wine Bottles*: Wines on the table or in a large wine cooler silver plated for the whites and the rosés.

Tip: You can use sea urchin looking objects and candles in the shape of seashells to spread around the table. Small sea lanterns can be placed on the table. You can also hook metal sea lanterns on branch trees.

Grillades Monte-Carlo Table Décor

—*Flowers*: You should buy flowers that are out of the ordinary and merit extra attention like birds of paradise, heliconia, ginger or pink lilies. You can also avoid flowers, and instead place small *plantes grasses*, or a micro lemon tree and micro orange tree.

—*Music*: Henri Salvador: Jazz Mediterranee, Jardin d'Hiver, Viktor Lazlo.

—*Scent and Candles*: Any candles of mimosa and gardenia will do the trick and envelop your guests with the mystique of the French Riviera.

Grillades Monte-Carlo *Apéritif*

—The Drink: The traditional non-alcoholic refreshing drink is a *citron pressé* (squeezed lemon with water and a bit of sugar) as well as dry white wines and rosés, which are all cooled in a large wine cooler full of ice. Do not forget to have a sufficient amount of ice.

—The *Aperitif nibbles:* On the table place some trays of crudités and dip, for your guests to nibble on in between the main dishes, (or while the host is starting to cook).

Grillades Monte-Carlo Menu

On one tray place two types of sauces: fresh mayonnaise, and a bowl of lemon juice, virgin olive oil and fresh herbs like dill, *herbes de Provence*, and pressed garlic all mixed together. Also add a box of gourmet sea salt.

The accent food is in the seafood: giant shrimps, *gambas*, sardines and *rougets* to begin with, followed by a large fish like a salmon or two types of fish or lobsters. You can cook them wrapped up in aluminum foil with a bit of lemon juice, olive oil and salt on top. Alternatively, or together, you can make fish *brochettes*.

To serve the fish, you can add fresh grilled vegetables such as fennels, zucchini, and peppers and a rice salad.

For dessert, you can gently grill fruits such as apricot and peaches and serve them with ice cream or *crème fraiche* (sour cream) and honey.

Very important! Do not forget the *rince doigts*, which is a bowl with lemon water for the guests to rinse their fingers as they will have used them with the shrimps and fish. Place them on the buffet or on a side table (the wheeled table is great for that) with small white napkins next to it. Also add several empty dishes to collect the shells and *brochette* sticks once they are used by your guests.

GRILLADE DU CHASSEUR AMBIANCE

Occasions

This ambiance is nice for informal events, such as gatherings with friends and family.

Why This Title?

We call it *Le Chasseur* ("The Hunter") because both the décor and the food will create a feeling of honesty and robustness, inviting nature at the table. This ambiance is recommended in autumn and winter.

Grillade du Chasseur Décor

The idea is to distill an atmosphere of authenticity.

—*Table:* Try to find a rustic wooden table. Just add a table runner in the middle of the table, in a deep rich color like burgundy or prune.

—*Tablecloth:* A rustic looking tablecloth will work well. As an alternative, you can also use placemats. Try to find a natural element motif to bring the nature onto the table in its rawness and simplicity such as a big leaf look-a-like, a straw, a cork or just a wooden mat.

—*Napkins:* Match them to the color of the table runner.

—*Cutlery:* Rustic hunting style or *Lagliole* style.

—*Glasses:* Strong rustic wine glasses, same color as the table runner. Use clear water goblets, both with no feet.

—*Plates:* Rustic looking plates or plates with a leaf or vegetable shape or just a large plate in slate. Regarding the side plates, they can be in slate if you use a vegetable shape porcelain plate, or in porcelain if you opt for the slate plate.

—*Butter Dish:* In sandstone, rustic looking, or if you have a large beautiful farmers market piece of butter, just place it on a white small plate. Sprinkle it with some gourmet sea salt and pepper.

—*Serving Dish*es and *Salad Bowl*s: Match to the rusticity and authenticity of the plates.

—*Rack bottle:* In a rack bottle you can place the olive oil, vinegar, pepper grinder, gourmet salt and in another rack bottle, you can place the red wines, beers, water bottles (both still and sparkling).

Bread pieces are served in a small paper bag already placed next to the plate or in a big basket for people to pick up.

Wines such as *Burgundy* or Sancerre for a lighter version are recommended. Beers like *Stella Artois.*

—*Flowers:* Wild tulips, eucalyptus leaves and artichokes leaves all placed in a wooden forest-looking vase or anything rustic.

—*Scent and candles:* Wooden frame candle holders with musk or wood scent candles.

Grillade du Chasseur *Apéritif*

—*The Drink*: Bloody Mary or a chilled red or white wine. Beers are great too for barbecue.

—*The Aperitif nibbles*: The apéritif is taking place while the host is starting to cook. On the table are rustic *canapés*, where you can place a couple of trays full of endive leaves arranged in a clockwork design, containing various dips. Do not forget to add slices of salami and French gherkins.

Grillade du Chasseur Menu

Starter:

You will also have various different kinds of French mustard served in their pots with a spoon (don't forget a tiny receptacle to hold the spoons once used). Dijon aux Grains and Estragon are some of the traditional flavors.

You can start by grilling different types of merguez sausages that are quite spicy or French sausages made out of boar or pork.

Main dish:

Either a main piece of meat like a *Côtes de Boeuf*, or opt for various meat *brochettes*, like duck *brochettes*.

You can serve two large fresh mushroom salads with chives (in a yogurt and mustard dressing) as well as a multi-layered salad. Potatoes are a must! They can be slowly cooked in the coal, as a baked potatoe, since the end of the *apéritif* and will be succulent with a touch of fresh butter or *crème fraiche* (sour cream) and parsley.

Dessert:

A *Camembert* cheese cooked in its box. Make sure to take the cheese out of the box first, take away the paper, put it back in the box and slowly cook it on the barbecue for a few minutes away from the center.

At the end, you can grill some *bananas flambé* with rum with vanilla ice cream.

CHAPTER 5

Happy Hour Ambiance

The Happy Hour ambiance in France is not related to the time spent with colleagues after work in a bar or a pub. It is more of a mini cocktail party held at home around wine and appetizers.

APÉRITIF DIN DIN AMBIANCE

Occasion

If you don't feel like hosting an entire dinner party for various reasons, this is the perfect compromise. A mini din-din is simply a cocktail party, but with a bit more food.

Why This Title?

An *Aperitif Din Din (or Aperitif Dinatoire)*, as we call it in France, is having drinks with a little food. It is a good method for introducing new friends to others or inviting newly made acquaintances to your inner circle without committing yourself too much by investing in a dinner.

It allows for a relaxed vibe amongst people, going around the room at your rhythm and leisure. It is also a good way to sort of "test" your visitors to see who would be a nice fit for the next dinner party you would likely host. Call it a pre-requisite training or even foreplay for things to follow! The mood is laid back and convivial, the food is salty and sweet and eaten with your hands. The *Apéritif Din Din* shouldn't last longer than two hours or so.

Our Experience

One of the celebrations which suits an *Apéritif Din Din* is the Beaujolais Nouveau! Every year, traditionally in late November, we rush to the liquor store to buy the Beaujolais freshly arrived and invite ten to twenty people over to celebrate. It is one of the easiest and most relaxing ways (or excuses) to entertain.

You will simply need some fruit and cheese. The Beaujolais wine (if that's what you choose) is served chilled with a beautiful selection of cheeses from mild to pungent, from goat to cow and from soft to hard.

The cheeses are displayed on different trays (wooden ones are perfect), served on wine leaves or straw. Open them at the last minute to avoid any strong unpleasant smells! Next to the cheese trays, you have the different types of breads (baguettes, flutes, *pain de campagne*, sesame, biscuits, etc.) placed in wicker baskets.

A tray of cut *crudités*, sliced apples and grapes and *le tour est joué, santé*!

Apéritif Din Din Table Setup

The preparation is *très* simple! Just drape your dining room table with a colored tablecloth (as oppose to a white tablecloth, in case you get some wine stains).

You will place all the glasses, including wine glasses as well as Champagne flutes and water glasses, to one side.

On the same side, lay out large Champagne buckets with ice. You can be creative and use other types of decorative containers as ice buckets. Your bottles of whites, Champagne or Prosecco will stay chilled that way. Don't forget to have an extra medium size container with ice for the guests.

—*Drink Layout:* The first row should contain red and white wines and the *crème* liquors such as *crème de cassis* or *crème de framboise* to mix with the white wine to make a *Kir.* Behind are all the liquors and the juices including gin, vodka, whiskey, *pastis*, tonics and fruit juices like tomato and pineapple juice. The water is kept seperately for an easy access. No cocktails should be prepared in advance. Place the vodka in the freezer until the last minute. And don't forget the corkscrews!

—*Food Layout:* On the other side, you will have all the plates and trays presenting the cheeses, fruits and *canapés* on it. Include the cut slices of lemon and the condiments for the drinks such as Worcestershire sauce and celery salt.

—*Tablecloth*: Any plain deep color will suit.

—*Napkins*: Paper napkins.

—*Glasses*: Bistro glasses.

Apéritif Din Din Décor

—*Flowers*: Colored lilies in deep red or yellow. Seasonal flowers in a central bouquet.

—*Music:* Brazilian Jazz and Afro-Jazz.

—*Scent and Candles:* Anything fruity.

Apéritif Din Din Menu

—Various *canapés* like smoked salmon on *blinis* with *crème fraiche*, *tartines* of *pâté* cut in squares on.

—Lightly toasted bread

—Salami slices

—Nuts like almonds and cashews

—Carrots and fennel sticks with salt and olive oil

—Cherry tomatoes

—Slices of quiche or mini pizzas

—Two large trays of cheese and crackers

—Sliced apple and grapes

PART II

THE PSYCHOLOGY TO CONNECT WITH OTHERS

When eating by yourself, you simply perform a physiological act. But as soon as you share that moment with someone, it becomes an opportunity to connect, it becomes an experience!

We know that connecting with people is not always easy, and being in the company of others can trigger tension. Whether it is a silence around the table plunging the host in a state of panic, desperately trying to come up with something light and funny to say, or dealing with an awkward conversation, a flawless connection might be harder than we think. However, it won't and shouldn't stop you from having fun.

CHAPTER 6

Be Aware of Your Mental Hiccups

For the most part, French families sit down at dinner time and enjoy regular family meals. It is fair to say that the frequency, due to today's constraints, has diminished, but it still plays a meaningful role in France. This tradition contains tons of social practice and constitutes an indispensable tool used later on in life, especially for children, insofar as helping them to navigate through the walks of social interaction.

Meals shared together provide the platform to talk about what happened during the day, on weekends, toss around various topics, helping the family to reframe, deal with conflict and adjust to the different situations. Experiencing the world of others, and actually hearing people, while forging a relationship with food is one of the nicest ways to practice getting comfortable socially.

The mobile and changing environment we live in, which often dictates the level and quality of our human interaction we have with people, desperately needs the grounding experience of sitting down, at home, around a meal with family and friends. Meals unite people. They bring us a sense of feeling alive.

But still, playing host may come with a bit of stress! It is more of an art form than a science, full of the unknown, yet beautiful.

Undoubtedly, throwing dinner parties at home hasn't always been a glitch-free experience for the both of us either, even if we are French, and we've learned quite a lot along the years. We'd like to share some of our mental hang-ups and attitudes as well as the ones of some of our close friends.

This section is especially dedicated to show you how to stay emotionally robust and host a fun dinner party. We will explain and clarify why we harbor these emotional roadblocks and provide you with solutions, so that not only will you be able to ride the wave as a pro, but also you will discover aspects about yourself that you didn't know existed. As a host, don't forget that you are the producer of your own event and that includes being in charge of your mental attitude!

Before delving deep into our psychological approach, let's break down four typical personality fears that we both encountered somehow at various times.

Host Personality Stereotypes

The Manic-Overachiever Host/Hostess

This is the adrenaline seeking, competitive type. A manic host is not the one seeking perfectionism; rather they have problems with time management because they think they could do it all. When this happens, they are cool as a cucumber the morning of the dinner party, doing sports or going to the spa, thinking that they have all the time in the world. Then two hours before the guests arrive, they become manic.

The Shy Host/Hostess

Shy people often crave social interaction, but avoid it for fear of criticism or rejection. They secretly want to shine but are reluctant to socialize. In terms of hosting, they are sometimes afraid of cooking something new, inviting new people into their homes, or worry about what they will talk about with their guests. They need to be in their comfort zone.

The Clueless Host/Hostess

This is for the host that has no ideas. They don't know what to cook, or whom to invite, or for what occasion—yet they're dying to host a dinner. They tend to either not think about the logistics and food, and then panic at the last minute, or they over-do it by buying ten different cookbooks and having too much to choose from.

The Host-Zilla

You know this type. The pressure-cooker. The perfectionist. This person has trouble delegating and usually spends too much time and money on a dinner party. This personality type tends to want to impress so much, that he or she will forget that the main point is to have a good time. Most "host-zillas" are multi-talented and organized (hence why they are perfectionists) but their need for perfection tends to override and may even ruin the dinner party.

Any way you want to look at it, when you decide to open the door to your home and into your kitchen, you also simultaneously reveal and expose parts of your personality. Think about it, unconsciously, when we add it all together, we expose our tastes in decoration, clothes, food choices, music and cars all the time. We send outward signals to the world on who we are, what we want to be validated for and how we want to be identified.

You can't help but wonder as to how one is perceived and experienced by others, prompting a constant internal dialogue on what's expected of us from other people, as well as fine tuning what each other's intentions are. Different emotions may resurface, prompted by old and tenacious fears in the form of negative self-talk, casting its shadow over our intentions. There is often a little voice telling us that we won't be up to standard, and that we will be made fun of—and by and large—will be judged negatively. Feelings of frustration, impatience, insecurity, panic and anxiety, can take center stage. Don't let these feelings block your mind and your heart. Feelings and thoughts are just transitory. They do not define who you are underneath. Some reactions to that anxiety can be detrimental and cause you to precipitate into a steep ravine of unease and defensiveness, hence spoiling the essence of what lies ahead: a pleasurable experience.

Given the four different personality types we outlined earlier, here is a more in-depth look at each of them, where we provide testimonials (stories that actually happened to us or people we know) and how we found a way to conquer our main hiccups.

Panic! They're Here!

This testimonial fits in with the "manic host/hostess" personality type:

This is Bahia's story:

Sometimes I can be a little competitive in life, which I've learned, can also signify that I may have a deep rooted insecurity, prompting me to work hard to prove my worth and impress others with my superiority, but let's not get into that! Sometimes competition is good because it challenges you to advance.

So my friend Chuckie and I are the only ones in our group of friends who regularly invite others over for dinner. Chuckie, a witty, clever banker who is just as competitive as me, thought that he could cook better than me using creative ideas. I, not as imaginative when it comes to cooking as he, but a top-notch *connaisseur* in the art of creating an ambiance, decided to compete with him. We would both host our own separate dinner parties and our friends would be the judges. My dinner was first.

Since my weakness is coming up with cool and creative dishes, I decided to make an effort and invest in some cooking books. I decided to make everything from a Jacques Pépin cook book:

Appetizer: Lobster in artichoke hearts

Entrée: Halibut on fresh polenta with pepper oil

Dessert: Chocolate fondant

My four guests were arriving at 7:30pm on a Saturday night. It was July. I thought that if I bought all of the food the day before, I was able to squeeze in a beach day Saturday morning, and make it back in time to cook dinner. The beach was almost a two-hour drive each way. My plan: leave at 8:30am, arrive at the beach at 10:30am, soak up some sun until 1pm, arrive back in the city at 3pm and have 4.5 hours to clean, cook, set the table, take a shower, etc. Plenty of time right?

Wrong. I had not anticipated enough time for cleaning my apartment and for cooking not one, not two, but three new dishes from scratch. Plus, I had forgotten a few last minute ingredients and the flowers, so I was rushing in and out of stores frantically, wasting precious time. One hour before my guests arrived, I had not even started cooking! To my chagrin, they arrived perfectly on time, and I was a nervous wreck when opening the door. I almost yelled at them for arriving on time! The food ended up being quite good, but it still could have been better. The big drawback, however, was not so much the food, it was the fact that I was totally not with my guests mentally. I wasn't even listening to them—there was no connection. Inside, I had a hundred billion thoughts and feelings. My anxiety was sky high and I thought that I would lose the competition and most importantly, not have fun. Plus I blew the only thing I knew how to do best, which was to create a cool atmosphere. When my friends left my apartment, I felt empty and depleted.

So what did I learn?

- Not to jam-pack lots of other activities in the same day, thinking that I could "do it all". Secretly, I wanted to prove that I could pull off an amazing dinner and also squeeze in a beach day too. That I was this omnipotent wonder woman. But the reality is that by over-scheduling my day, not allotting adequate time to prepare for the dinner party, I had the "excuse" of throwing an unsuccessful dinner. It was actually self-sabotage, camouflaged with a wonder woman costume.
- That there's no need to prove your self-worth through a dinner party. My friends like me for who I am, period.
- To buy all of the food and clean my apartment the day before the dinner party. I should have set my deadline of having everything and a clean apartment at 2pm, the day of the dinner party.
- To not cook three dishes from scratch, especially if I'm not familiar with them. I should have concentrated on one main dish, the *entrée*, made a nice salad for the appetizer, and bought a tart for the dessert.
- To enjoy the experience of preparing new dishes, as much as experiencing the dinner party itself. In fact, if you leave yourself a few hours to calmly prepare the food, you might actually enjoy it. It can be therapeutic. Then, one hour before the guests arrived, I would have played some music, poured myself a glass of wine, placed the *hors d'oeuvres* in the living room, splashed on some perfume and lip-gloss, and relaxed.

If I would have taken even one of these tips, my stress level would have been reduced and I would not have appeared as manic as I was. We never found out who won the dinner competition, but something tells me that he did.

I'm Not Good Enough and They'll Find Out!

This testimonial fits in with the "shy host/hostess" personality type:

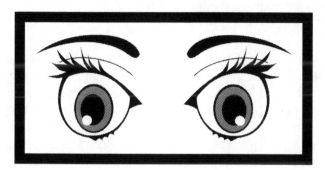

This is our friend Amanda's story:

Amanda is in her early thirties and is one of the kindest people we know. She is shy but her husband, Marc, is not. He loves to have people over all the time, and she doesn't. Marc is often inviting new and old guests over because it helps him relax after a long week of work (he travels a lot). So about once a month, Marc throws a dinner party at their house. While he thinks it's the best idea since sliced bread, Amanda dreads it.

Why does Amanda feel this way?

"I dread it because there's too much pressure to 'perform' where I have to force myself to be extroverted, which I'm just not. For years, I had to put on a smile and pretend that it was fun. It just wasn't fun for me. I felt fake when I made too much of an effort, because it wasn't me, and then again, I felt useless and invisible when I was being myself. So I felt like I was dammed if I was being myself, and dammed if I was *not* being myself".

"Marc is naturally out-going; he can have anyone over and it doesn't matter to him. For me, I'm comfortable with my friends and family, but it takes me a little while to get to know new faces. So I'm terrorised when Marc invites new people. It's manageable when he's in the room, but if he drifts off to another room and leaves me alone with the guests, I don't know what to talk about. Plus, I'm always thinking that they will talk about me behind my back, after they leave. That they didn't like the food, that the wine was not chilled enough, that the tablecloth was not ironed enough, that I looked fat, etcetera. And Marc just doesn't understand why I'm putting so much pressure on myself".

But Amanda learned to conquer her fears.

She remained unspoken about these anxieties to her husband for the first two years of marriage. After the third year, however, she had had enough. Amanda decided to confront her hubby and communicate why she felt the way she did. So they reached a compromise, where they could both be satisfied. Marc agreed to invite less people, fewer than eight to be specific, and make the dinners more cosy and casual and less formal. That would take a significant amount of pressure off of Amanda regarding the expectations of cooking for formal occasions—plus—having less people was just easier. Amanda could actually talk to most of them and feel good about being her real self. She no longer felt like a fraud. And Marc was happy because he still got to have his monthly dinner parties.

So what did we learn?

- Communicate. If you're feeling so much pressure to entertain at home, don't wait years to voice it to your partner. Don't be afraid to show your fears and vulnerabilities. We all have them and they need to be addressed and not swept under the carpet. Dealing with them will help to solve your problem.
- Accept yourself. If you're more shy than others, so what? It doesn't mean there's something wrong with you, or that you can't host a dinner your way. *Au contraire*, shy people are usually really good listeners and are compassionate beings, therefore more attentive to their guests.
- Remember, people don't really think about you, they think about themselves. Don't be fooled. If you think your guests are judging you, know that they are just as equally afraid that you will judge them.
- Be comfortable with uncertainty. Your relationship with uncertainty is a measure of how successful you will become. Slowly learn to step outside of your comfort zone. Try new sports or hobbies, cook different meals, or take a different route to work, whatever. The more you slowly come out of your comfort zone, the more you will grow and you will accept new people and circumstances into your life.

Lost in Translation

This testimony fits in with the "clueless host/hostess" personality type:

This is our friend David's story:

David is a charming man. A true romantic at heart. When he first laid eyes on Monica, he knew she was the one. They started dating and when time came for David to bring their relationship to the next level and become exclusive, he wanted to prepare something special for her. He wanted to seal the deal, so to speak, in declaring her to be his girlfriend. So, what to do?

He thought about it for days.

Should he organize a helicopter ride over the New York skyline? Too over the top.

Should he invite her to a nice restaurant, followed by the theatre? A little boring.

Should he write her a short poem and send her flowers? Cheesy.

Should he take her sky diving to make it really memorable? Yikes.

And then he had the "aha" moment. David could cook her a nice homemade dinner, all by himself. It would show his devotion without being over the top, boring, cheesy or scary. And it would impress her. But what to cook?

Now the agony begins . . .

One week prior to the dinner, David searches the Internet. The more he searched, the more he got confused. Every time he saw a dish, either the photo looked great, but the recipe was as understandable as the Da Vinci Code, or alternatively, the dishes looked simple, but had no corresponding photos, so he couldn't imagine how it would look like. David then decided to go to the bookstore and invest in a cookbook. But the bookstores had three full rows of cookbooks alone! There were hundreds of French, Italian, Vegetarian, Pan-Asian, and Moroccan cookbooks with all their variations: healthy, rich, energetic, vegan, for appetizers, desserts, BBQs, the list was endless. There was a superfluous amount to choose from. Feeling overwhelmed and anxious just two days before the dinner, David ran out of the bookstore and called his mother.

His mother, not knowing what culinary advice to give him, gave him some heartfelt wisdom: "Honey, it doesn't matter what you cook for her, as long as you show her you made an effort. You will figure it out. Just don't forget to clean the apartment, buy some champagne, buy a good bottle of French red wine, and add a little bouquet of flowers. That alone will touch her".

David was relieved but not cured. He still didn't know what to cook.

But as luck would have it, he was now completely aware of what his challenges were, so he kept his eyes opened, probably subconsciously. On his walk home, he passed by the home goods store called *Sur La Table*. Now on any given day, he would walk past this store not looking twice at it. But this time was different, so he decided to venture in. And there, in two minutes, voilà, David found his answer: "I'll make her fondue!"

He bought the set, and then googled how to make both cheese and chocolate fondue. It was relatively easy, and the two fondues would really impress Monica! Plus it's romantic because you share the food together. And another plus is that chocolate is an aphrodisiac! Genius he thought.

David was now no longer clueless but very confidant. The dinner was a success and Monica was floored. But the anxiety that fell over him for the two weeks leading to the dinner were filled with confusion and anxiety.

So what did David learn from this experience?

- That it's the thought that counts. The act of making an effort alone would please his girlfriend. Not the brouhaha of going all out and losing your main purpose, which is to please a loved one.
- That sometimes, less is more.
- That it was useless to have spent two weeks fussing over it, causing him so much anxiety. Whenever you feel too much anxiety, it usually means something is wrong. Listen to your body when it communicates to you these fears and worries, and shift gears.
- That love is the best ingredient to a successful and intimate dinner.

It's GOTTA be the Best!

This testimonial fits in with the "host/zilla" personality type:

This is Anne's story:

Many years ago I hosted a dinner to meet my future in-laws. The stakes were high and I wanted to impress them. I wanted them to see me as a godly, kind, gorgeous, talented, intelligent, mesmerizing hostess and future wife. I wanted to look like Cindy Crawford and cook like Martha Stewart. I wanted them to be blown away and love me. So everything had to be planned out perfectly.

What made it particularly difficult for me was not knowing what to expect. I didn't know who these people were really, or what they liked, or if they were nice, or if they would judge me, etcetera. I had no clue as to their food likings or their openness. My fiancé, like most men, fed me the bare minimum amount of information.

In my organization, I had a military style checklist:

I. THE FOOD

- Hors d'oeuvres
- Appetizers
- Entrée
- Cheese
- Dessert
- Tea/Coffee

II. THE DECOR
III. FLOWERS
IV. CONVERSATION TOPICS
V. PRACTICING INTRODUCING MYSELF IN FRONT OF MIRROR
VI. MY OUTFIT
VII. MY BACK-UP OUTFIT
VIII.SPA DAY THE DAY BEFORE DINNER PARTY
IX. IMMACULATE HOUSE + PERFECT DECOR

But it didn't just stop at making a list—it took over my life as I was going to war.

I literally wrote a twenty-page report to prepare for the event. Yes, I was crazy! Every chapter was clearly defined. The "Decor" chapter involved purchasing a new coffee table on-line, and buying new linens and silverware. The "Flowers" were also deeply researched. I needed to know the hidden symbolism behind different flowers, and how they would combine together for the three sets of bouquets I would custom order from my florist. For the "Spa" chapter, I needed to give a down payment for the spa treatment, which included a deep tissue massage, seaweed wrap, facial, and mani-pedi. All of the other chapters were outlined with the same rigor and preciseness. There was even a chapter that was not included but which consumed a large part of my schedule: the daily workouts for fifteen straight days to get the perfect body in time for the dinner party.

Now what was the end result? And how did the dinner party go?

The end result was this:

—I spent in total $2,000 on one night. Money I could have saved for a new car down payment, or for my retirement, or for my future children's education.

—I was yelling and screaming at every vendor for not being professional enough. Literally everyone. The online sales operators, the florist, the butcher, the hair dresser, the taxi drivers, the cleaners, even the dog walkers on the street who were walking too slowly.

—My fiancé was literally non-existent to me for at least a week prior to the event. I don't even remember talking to him.

—My work was neglected.

As for the dinner party. Well—let's just say that I was not at my most elegant.

Although the final checklist was pretty much on target the day of the dinner party, the only thing racing through my mind in those final hours were, "the ETA is in 90 minutes—the ETA is in 60 minutes—the ETA is in 20 minutes—the ETA is in 5 seconds: SHIT"!

I'll get to the point right now. The dinner party was good and the in-laws enjoyed themselves. But here is the grey part: I think I went too far with the food choices. I gave them too many choices for everything. There were five different *hors d'oeuvres*, then the appetizers, then two choices of meats, seven different cheeses from three different countries (I wanted to show to them how cultured and international I was), and two desserts. Clearly it showed that I was trying too much. And that was just the food. Thank goodness they didn't know that I actually wrote a business plan, spent a ton of money and drove myself insane with the workouts and everything else!

Although the dinner party was a success on paper—and in this case literally—it actually wasn't a success. Why? Because I didn't listen to them, I didn't ask them any questions, and I was very stressed. The fact that I handled this dinner as if I were about to wage a war, "Operation Perfect Dinner Party", was ridiculous. I learned that inside, deep inside, I was actually waging a war with myself. A war to be perfect and do everything myself from beginning to end. And I've learned now, that there's no reason to create this inner turmoil. It simply is not worth it.

The good news is that ever since this dinner party, I have learned to delegate and relax a lot more with all my dinner parties throughout the years.

What did I learn?

- That it is not about getting "everything right" but instead focus on what matters most: sharing a good time with people you choose to invite.
- To keep in check my tendencies of being impatient, fastidious, focusing on the 2% that might go wrong, and refusing people's help.
- That there is no such thing as "perfect" and adopt a more rounded philosophical approach.
- To speak with a reformed perfectionist over a glass of wine and laugh about the whole thing! There's just something so wonderful about getting support and identifying with someone similar.

Unexpected Disasters—Ooh La La!

"A host is like a general: calamities often reveal his genius."

—Horace

In this instance, the failure of the dinner party is not caused by the negative attitude of the host but rather by an unpredictable variable. In a situation like this, the host has the superb opportunity to display and deploy, first by her stoic attitude, then by her rapidity of reaction, and how she can conjure the unexpected without being engulfed by it. The answer lies in her resilience and her sense of humour; which are the two allies of this type of challenge. The host will make her guests grow even fonder of her, if something goes unexpactantly wrong and she makes the best of it. It will imprint, on the minds of the guests, a memorable evening.

These two stories illustrate the point perfectly.

Francoise's girlfriend named Daniele:

Her husband had invited six important guests from the town hall to their country house. It was a bit of a last minute invitation. She had to rush to the local *traiteur* (gourmet shop) and by chance found an already freshly cooked meal. A bit overpriced and very big for the size of her oven she thought, but the short notice left her with little choice. She had enough in the pantry to offer a delicious starter and needed some cheeses and fresh bread to complete her dinner menu. All well.

When it was time to eat the main dish, she walked into the kitchen, extracted the large glass dish with difficulty from the oven, and trotted back with triumph to the table . . . when BOOM! As she was reaching for the corner of the table, the heavy glass dish split itself into two, pouring the entire boiling food in the middle of the rug! It was a mix of surprise, shame and total embarrassment. Covered with meat pieces all over her outfit, she rapidly brushed it from her dress, and exploded in a nervous laugh that went viral among the guests. She saved the dinner by using her humor, followed by cooking up a nice bowl of spaghetti.

Anne's oven betrayal!

I had reached a learning curve ever since a stupid episode taught me to always verify my kitchen appliances—something that for years I took for granted. Let me explain:

My husband had invited two major clients and their spouses to a French dinner at home. Back then, one of my most reliable dishes for elegant dinners was to cook a beautiful sea bass in the oven. I felt completely in control and relaxed having prepared this dish numerous times before. It was safe and predictable.

To my shock and horror though, that day, both my ovens broke. It was 7:45pm, the guests were happy in the living room finishing their *apéritif*, and exchanging the usual polite conversation. Petrified, powerless and fuming, I kept pacing my kitchen like a caged animal. How could this be, was it a dark spell from the universe? When chaos strikes, one has to get creative and pray for luck. So I decided to make a *bouillabaisse*. I knew I had some frozen seafood at the bottom of the freezer. My luck was starting to turn, in my favour, I thought. Except that it would take another hour! Discouraged but not vanquished yet, I filled up small plates with more quail eggs, a pyramid of olives and nuts in the hope that it would gain me some time. My husband rushed to the cellar and brought enough white wine to relax everybody for another hour. And get them a bit tipsy of course. At 10:00pm, we finally served dinner. While uncovering our new hot and steamy dish, we all discovered various heads and pieces of seafood floating along the potatoes. As I was serving each of my guests, I was silently hoping that nobody would notice, or that no one would know how to make the traditional recipe—which is a recipe that is rich in the tradition of Marseilles (in the south of France).

So as we say in France, *"quand le bateau chavire, on garde le sourire"*! Which vaguely translates as "when the boat sinks, we keep on smiling". But aside from surviving this incident and others, the focus should be on having a great time and riding the wave of the unexpected disaster.

CHAPTER 7

Psychological Tools to Win Your Audience

"Attitude is a little thing that makes a big difference."
—Winston Churchill

To be ultra-confident has nothing to do with a set of techniques and everything to do with attitude.

Chemistry with new people, in our experience, often happens when we least expect it. Our best memories derive from completely unexpected connections with people.

Being in the company of others is, for the French, very much imbued with seduction, a sort of *raison d'*être, lodged in many corners of human exchange. It is not intended to achieve anything, or to get to anything like a sexual conquest or a date. Rather, it resembles more of a fun *passe-temps*. It is, in many ways, how people like to relate to one another. The dinner party is no exception, and in fact, it is a big seductive enterprise, which in some ways superficially masks the anxiety that we may feel in other's company. Showing your interest for someone is highly seductive for the other person and helps relax the atmosphere. Once again, we are not talking about seducing for a sexual purpose, but to make the other feel special. Being seductive, passionate and confident is an essential ingredient of human communication and an amazing tool to facilitate one's curiosity and movement toward the other, in order to create a real exchange full of reciprocity.

Far from just nourishing the body, the meal is an instrument of enticement aimed at providing a sensual gratification. From dressing up your table, to arranging your hair, to the scent of candles or the voice and conversation, it is all there to titillate the people with subtle challenges. This aspect can help understand, in part, why French people like so much to get together around a meal and share that experience. Social interaction may, as we have seen, represent a minefield, but it can also be great fun. It is the perfect opportunity to express your individuality and be stylish at the same time!

As you are offering a glass of Champagne or serving food, always stay open to your surroundings by psychologically placing yourself in the room—not in your head worrying about things. Open yourself to the experience that is unfolding.

Your challenge is to find your own emotional cocktail between a sense of feeling safe, while at the same time, being comfortable with a certain level of uncertainty and the unknown.

How to Feel Safe.

What makes us feel safe is anything that covers predictability and reliability. You can achieve that by making sure that everything we talked about earlier is ticked. That will bring a sense of order and serenity.

Make sure to review what values are being satisfied when you are throwing a dinner party. What aspect of yourself does it enable you to express: The generous you? The nourishing you? The aesthetic you? The theatrical you? Is it honoring friendship, family, effort, beauty? You will feel better and more grounded about yourself by throwing into the world what you hold dear and what will be in alignment with these values.

How to Be Open to the Unknown.

As we mentioned earlier, there is always a level of anticipation and anxiety at not knowing precisely how things will turn out—but that's precisely what makes it exciting. It is the creative aspect that you are dealing with and that makes it interesting. Don't give up too much just to feel safe, allow some unpredictability and mystery to take place. When we step forward and encounter someone, we jump into a magic circle, a shared space co-created by the two people. That space is where the dance of being with someone begins. It is about taking turns at offering and accepting, at leading and following—with balance.

It is not a space to be used for narcissistic gratification where the other becomes an evaluation tool on how amazing you are or any other social comparison. Don't be hesitant at connecting with others. Let the protective masks fall down as the warmth of human connection diffuses its soft power. It will help you feel less like you're in a performance role, and more authentic. Deep down we are all longing for connection.

The 10 Ways to Harness Your Confidence and Feel Alive: Va VaVoum!

From the delicate balance between safety and uncertainty, here are some further suggestions to harness the confident attitude, and experience pleasure by connecting with others:

1. **De-center from yourself.**

Don't you feel that most of the time, we focus our attention and agonize over what will make us feel uncomfortable instead of what would make the other comfortable? We are locked in our minds; we're too self-absorbed.

In doing so, we miss and fail at connecting with the person next to us. We become absent and cut off. When we are sliding towards achievement and truthfully toward over-achievement in order to control how we want to be perceived, the rest of the human connection fades away from our awareness.

Instead, take charge by intentionally de-centering yourself and travel toward the other in an attempt to connect. Pick up on their energy. By this welcomed source of attention and energy coming from you, your guests will start to feel comfortable, trusting a bit more and gradually they will open-up. In turn, as you are witnessing their steady openness, feeling heard and understood, it will also increase your own sense of trust at sharing and increase your own sense of safety.

2. **Be curious like on a first date.**

Be interested in the person you're talking to, and look interested by looking at them in a new light. Remember when you met someone for the very first time who you really liked? You were interested in everything they were saying, weren't you? Every word uttered from the other person's mouth was reciprocated with excitement and awe. There is a sense of mystery and surprise weaved in with naivety and wonder. Try to put yourself in that frame of mind. Don't view them as if you know everything about them, and certainly don't judge them. There is no need to be over the top and take this tip literally, but just add a fresh coat of "getting to know you" to your dinner guests—even with people you know very well.

3. Exude your charisma and look the person in the eyes.

Get interested wholeheartedly into what the person says and is passionate about. That will dispense your sense of confidence and charisma. Also, look in the eyes of the person you are talking to. It will instantly give recognition and interest to the person. Your gaze will speak volumes before you've even moved your lips. Don't forget that body language is a huge chunk of communication. Looking into someone's eyes will make them feel like the center of your attention and in turn, will make you come across as charismatic and charming. Think of the charismatic actor or president who has the talent of always making their friend feel like they are the most interesting person in the room.

4. Keep it mysterious.

The trick is to generate curiosity in the other person and tease his or her imagination rather than being always factual and technical. You are not there to tell the guests your entire life story, and you are not there to conduct a business presentation or an interview. The operative word here is playful!

5. Be seductive by mastering the art of conversing.

Lots of us are scared at the idea of not knowing what to talk about, or worse, if suddenly silence invades the dinner table! Then what? Whether you're an alpha or a beta, here are a few simple back-up conversation starters that always work:

—How is work? This will lead to another topic, like talking about a certain industry.

—If you had a $100 million, what would you do with the money besides solving world hunger (which is a bit of a cheesy reply actually)? We love this question because the person has no idea it's coming, and usually answers with depth, which leads to a whole slew of other conversations.

—How do you know so and so? A classic that always works.

—What was the craziest thing you have ever eaten? A light question that never hurt anyone.

Conversing is one of the oldest and most powerful seduction tools. It will be the salt of your dinner because along with your food and your sensuous ornaments, an affable voice will stimulate and tease the mind. Without digressing too much, we all know that the biggest sex organ is the brain! In fact *l'esprit* is what Frenchmen and Frenchwomen enjoy playing at. It is part of seducing someone. So, as part of your seduction kit, use engaging, lively and amusing conversations, because, let's not forget, the point of a dinner party is to expand your topics and to exchange ideas—and learn from each other.

When you listen to what the other person says, do not cut off your attention by thinking about what kind of clever answer you'll come up with. When you're thinking of what to say next, you tend to not listen to the other person. Instead, just attend to what is being said. When the guest is finished, you can paraphrase what has been said or mirror the feeling expressed by the person. You can start some of your replies with yes, and it will convey a sense of inclusion and welcome. You can also ask follow-up questions to find out more about what they are saying as it promotes the development of the dialogue and confirms your interest in the person. Remember, you are talking with someone, not to someone!

Have confidence that others will bring something positive and interesting to the table, because they usually do! Having said that, be careful not to stay too long with the same person either and create a mini *tête-à-tête* amongst the rest of your guests! There is a fine line between spreading yourself too thinly amongst all your guests, and spending the whole evening talking to only one person.

Also, try not to engage in adversarial conversation, but rather engage with the dance movement of a reciprocal exchange.

As a rule of thumb, do not get pressured into being the erudite entertainer or the comic of the year. It is not a performance but a way to connect with fellow human beings. Simply enjoy being with the person you're talking to. Do not see conversations as a means to an end.

Ice-breaker topics include background information that you exchange with people you don't know like: school, children, job industry, sports and weather. The idea here is to see if you have any experiences in common and to get to know a bit more about the people you will share the dinner with. Keep it light and do not insist on any sort of achievement or any bragging.

6. Bridge the gap between the ideal you and the real you.

Have the courage to be your true self in the sense that being true to yourself is in being in alignment with your values. At its heart rests our need to feel accepted for who we are. The happy medium would look like a mix of the person you are subjectively expected to be, and the person you think you really are inside. Stop trying to control how you will be judged. It will only fuel your fears and doubts. Thoughts like, "I am not a good enough wife, mother, employee, cook, etc" . . . because at the end of the day, you cannot choose or control how you will be perceived.

7. Reconnect with your senses and desires for pleasure.

Pleasure provides us with that unique taste of vitality, closeness and aliveness as well as safety. However, on a closer look, it might not be experienced as straightforward as it ought to be, whereby some level of ambivalence can creep in, leaving us hesitant and shy at grabbing pleasure forcefully. Why is that?

- First, it is unusual, and when we experience it, we feel unprepared or overwhelmed by its intensity, so we choose not to create situations that will make us happy (unconsciously).
- Second, we are not sure we deserve it, because we might not be that good of a person, otherwise we would have received it and enjoyed it constantly throughout our life and we have not.

On top of that, very often we have been used to hearing that we have to work hard to obtain pleasure and happiness. We have to earn it. Remember those phrases: "don't be too happy", "if it looks too good to be true—it usually is", and "be careful, be careful".

Hopefully knowing that will help you to plug into that sea of energy commencing from the elaboration of your dinner party to the actual here and now experience in every day life. Pleasure is a good thing and a birthright. Don't feel guilty!

Taking the time to prepare food for someone is one of the most ancestral and profound human experiences. It is sensuous and comforting and goes far beyond just quenching the appetite. It also nourishes the soul. A dinner party is the occasion to re-conquer your relationship with your senses and the dizziness of pleasure you and your guests will experience.

As a host, before anyone has arrived, instead of worrying or feeling anxious, refocus on your senses by drawing pleasure from all the logistical activities such as arranging the table. Enjoy setting up all the sensuous temptations such as the scent of candles, the colors of the bouquet, the elegance of the tablecloth, the shininess of the glasses or the melody of a song—all in place for your guests to later slowly succumb and enjoy themselves.

Start bonding with the food.

As you are absorbed in the sensuality of the here and now, you will be in a delightful mood for when your guests arrive and be ready to guide them in a voluptuous atmosphere where their senses will be excited, teased and stimulated.

8. Harness your little negative voice.

Wrestle it to the ground. Self-talk is what you say to yourself about yourself. It usually takes the form of an absolutist decree such as I can't, I won't, it's crazy, etc. You can't get rid of it, but you can change your relationship with it.

One way to do this is to reframe the focus of your question.

If you frame your questions in a negative way such as "why can't I do this?", you formally invite your nasty little voice to come with plenty of answers as to why you can't.

- Because you're not good enough at cooking or dressing up.
- Because you didn't practice enough.
- Because you're too stupid, old, fat, skinny, shy and so on.

The more you focus on the negative, the more it is likely to happen. Instead, switch to questions asking for solutions such as: "how can I do this"—this way, you are focusing on the possibilities and solutions instead of the limitations. Also, focus on what you have instead of what you don't have.

Think of what is going right instead of concentrating on what is or could be going wrong. Again, it's all about your attitude and it is your choice to have the right attitude—or not.

9. You are not responsible for everything! Trust your guests.

> *"It is not so much our friend's help that helps us, as the confidence of their help."*
>
> —Epicurus

You've set up all the delicious props, so it's also time for your guests to rise to the occasion. Just stay invested mindfully in having fun, staying true to your individuality and confident in your own way. After that, let the music flow naturally. After all, you've done the best you could.

10. Relax and allow for some margin of messiness in the house.

The key element to a delightful and outstanding dinner party is not a perfect recipe, a perfect décor, or a perfect home. It is that *YOU,* the host enjoys it too. So don't worry about the normal aftermath mess such as the stack of dirty plates, pots an pans lying around, or the wine stain on the table cloth. The idea is to be more present at the dinner party, and stay in the 'Here and Now'. You can worry about the dishes after the guests leave. If you start cleaning up your kitchen while your guests are still there, you will be taking time away from the entire experience and the special event. Yes, you will gain time in cleaning for the next day, but just realize that you'll also be taking time away from connecting with others. And we have found that the best time of the dinner, is after the dinner. When everyone has eaten, everyone has now gotten to know each other, and everyone is relaxed. There's usually a wonderful vibe after the dinner, when the more real and authentic conversations take place. Why ruin it to do the dishes?

General Tips:

—Be scared and do it anyway, because most of the time it is your negative self-talk that is blurring your vision, and you are way overdramatic for what the situation calls for. Get out of your comfort zone and try to shine.

—Trust your inner resilience by being confident that when something unpredictable happens, you have the resources in you to deal with it. And even if you don't, it will be ok. Our fears are always worse than the reality or what could be—remember that.

—Share what you are passionate about.

—Never lose your temper.

—Do not check your Blackberry/iPhone (unless you are in the bathroom).

Before heading to the kitchen, make sure that your guests are talking to one another. You don't want to make them feel uncomfortable without you. If there is a conversation void, and even if you don't know what to say yourself, then go back to the previous conversation and add a question or comment to it. No big deal.

—Speak clearly, and try not to speak too much, especially when others— your guests—want to say something and express themselves.

PART III

LOGISTICS 1-0-1

This segment outlines your indispensable kit for each of your dinner parties. You will use it for all of the different ambiances (in Part I of this book). It lists all the particular elements that, once put together, will enable the host to feel empowered and in control. Every woman should have a little black dress as a basic item. Once you have the dress, you can add different jewellery, shoes, purses, scarves, and so on depending on your mood and the season. The same idea applies to this section.

To take another example: Imagine an artist with all of his or her different hues, paint and brushes and the imagination needed to create *un objet d'art*. The canvas is blank and requires you to share your own style, your own identity, and your own uniqueness.

The protocol is flexible and the rules are intended only to help you reveal your creativity and self, rather than imposing a rigid structure.

CHAPTER 8

Laying the Table . . . One, Two, Three!

The Table

Sitting around a table to share a meal is an ancestral ritual. The very shape of the table subtly starts to convey some atmosphere and gently sets the tone. For instance, a round shape is usually convivial and flexible while a rectangular table is a bit more structured, formal and hierarchical. The fundamental point here is that the emphasis is on feeling comfortable and relaxed regardless of the atmosphere you're choosing. Many variations from the two classic table types are also possible, such as joining two tables together, using a bar with stools which is more informal and allows everyone the freedom to change seats or just sitting on the living room floor around a coffee table, allowing for a very relaxed atmosphere. The choice is yours.

Table Linens

There are two major categories of table linens. The first category is white linens, in high quality cotton, either plain or embroidered. For example, you can have silver or gold embroidery if your celebration is for the holidays. The second category is colored linens, which vary depending on the ambiance. For example, a dark rich red or purple prune are very chic, while pink or gilded yellow are for warm and cosy times. Pastels are charming and romantic while vibrant green and bright yellow are good for the outdoors or the countryside.

Napkins

Napkins should match well with the choice of tablecloth. For formal occasions, they should preferably be in cotton. Otherwise nice paper napkins are fine. The napkins should be either folded into the main wine glass, placed on the side of the plate or on top of the plate.

Plates

Do not mix and match the plates. It's better to keep them uniform. If they cannot be uniform, then try to keep them consistent for each of the courses. If you have eight guests and only have enough white plates for the appetizer and *entrée*, then either wash the appetizer plates and use them for the dessert, or use other color/style plates just for the dessert. As an exception to the rule, you can use mix and matched plates for the *Normandie* ambiance by combining various vintage looking faience plates together (Chapter 1).

Each plate set design should have accompanying small appetizer plates and dessert plates, plus a main serving dish and a deeper dish for soups or other liquid dishes. In France, we rarely use small bread plates. This is more of an Anglo-Saxon tradition. The French, believe it or not, place their bread on the table itself. If we do put our bread on the plate, we tend to place the bread on the top left corner of our plate.

In general, you should have at least two different sets for entertaining. The first should be in porcelain for formal occasions, and the second and more basic, for all the casual ambiances, as well as for everyday use. The more sets you have, the more creative you can be with your table decoration. However, it is better to have a twelve piece set in one design, rather than a six piece set in four different designs.

Serving Platters and Dishes

As far as the serving dishes are concerned, the typical set for serving platters consists of four pieces:

- One flat round serving platter.
- One flat covered oval or covered casserole dish, preferably in cast iron or ceramic.
- One salad bowl (large).
- One rectangular or casserole-shaped dish, that is oven-safe.

It's better to buy these in a solid color that matches everything, like white. Also, for the oven-safe dishes, we strongly recommend investing in two good quality and elegant oven dishes as they will last for years (particularly for dishes that are hard to remove from the oven dish and that need to be served directly to your guests).

One could be used for the formal ambiances (porcelain, which is not oven safe) and the other for the casual ones (metal or ceramic, which is oven safe).

Glassware

You should have three basic sets of glassware that include:

- Wine glasses
- Water glasses
- Champagne flutes

Depending on how much you want to invest, you can indulge in specific wine glasses. For example, some people choose to have a set of white and red wine glasses.

You can also add some colored glasses for fun. Color is always fun! However, these types of wine glasses are generally used for the more casual wines or for very dry white wines in an intimate and romantic setting. For formal ambiances, only use clear wine glasses.

Since glasses should be consistent (meaning, there should be one type of each glass on the table) and since they tend to break easily, we recommend owning twelve of each set. While setting the table, you should place your glasses in this order, from left to right:

- Champagne flute
- Wine glass
- Water glass

Another interesting glass is the low or high cut martini glass that can be used during the *apéritif.* Martini glasses can also be used for many desserts such as fruit salads, sorbets, ice cream and chocolate mousse.

Water & Wine Carafes, Plus Ice Buckets

Carafes should only be used for tap water and ordinary table wines. Nice water bottles could be presented on the table directly, as well as any *terroir* wine bottles.

White wines should be kept in an ice bucket or elegant wine cooler—if possible.

Any red wines that are served a bit chilled, like a red Sancerre, Gamay, or Beaujolais, can be kept in an ice bucket up until the *hors d'oeuvres* are finished. Then they can be taken out and placed on the table so they will be at the perfect serving temperature.

For a good quality wine, like a *Bordeaux* or *Bourgogne*, for instance, the wine should be de-corked a little while before serving, allowing it to breathe. The better the bottle is, the more you want to display it on the table. There is no need for a decanter.

Flatware

If you can, invest in a good flatware storage chest. It is always a good item to have and makes for a lovely wedding gift.

Much like the rest of the essentials, the quantity and quality of flatware and cutlery depends on the ambiance. However, a good rule of thumb is to have:

- Two different forks (one large, one small)
- Two different knives (one large, and one small for fish)
- Two different spoons (one large, one small)
- Cheese knives
- Serving utensils

Other Accessories

Trolley or Tray table:

This is not a must have item, but it is quite practical when trying to avoid too many trips to the kitchen. The little side table has a top and a bottom and could be of any size provided it's not too big. It should be placed in the dining area and can be covered with a small tablecloth or solid color placemats (preferably white so it doesn't stand out too much from your main dining table décor).

This is a strategic piece as it allows you to easily access any dishes or refills. For example, if the main table is tight with too much food or too many people, the trolley could hold some of the food almost at an arm's length away from the dining table. It is useful for refills (such as extra bread, sauces, condiments, wine, and side dishes). On the lower level of the trolley is space to stack some dirty dishes that you may also not have room for in the kitchen. The trolley should be placed near the host or hostess.

Bread Basket:

According to the style of the dinner you choose the host, the bread basket could range from silver, to metal, to wicker or even to cotton. It is good to have at least one on hand.

Vases:

First of all, it is always nice to have a lot of flowers in your living and dining area, as flowers easily add color and aroma to the environment. We recommend having three vases, one for long stem and one for short stem flowers, and a third random one of your choice for extra flowers that guests might bring for you. If you're going to place one vase bouquet at the center of your table, be sure that it won't block the view from your guests. In fact, you should always use small vases for the table décor.

Candle Holders:

Candlesticks with tall taper candles are always pleasant and perfect for the dinner table. Choose white tapers for formal ambiances and colored tapers for casual or festive affairs. Low light candle pots are not flattering for one's complexion; however tea light holders with floating candles are perfect to spread out on the table. If you have a candelabra, either place it on a nearby console or make sure that it is high enough on the dining table so that the candles do not burn your guests. Burning your guest's hair would—without a doubt—ruin your dinner party! Candleholders can be in glass, ceramic, metal, or in a lantern shape.You can find them in many different sizes.

Trays:

These are useful for *hors d'oeuvres* at *aperitif* time, as well as for coffee at the end of a meal. Always place a white cotton napkin at the bottom unless the design corresponds to the selected ambiance. A napkin will also avoid having your glasses and cups slide from side to side.

We recommend having one large and one small tray (and out of these, one formal and the other casual). You could also buy a medium sized wooden (wicker) tray for a nice cheese presentation.

Individualized Tableware:

The purpose of the mini tableware is to transform something normal into an upgraded status. Placing your food in a mini ramekin, a mini casserole dish or a mini tagine dish, positioned in the middle of the plate, will bring that instant smile to your guest's faces because it is adorable! A mini saucer for the vinaigrette or gravy can also be added to some courses and poured individually.

Menus:

Depending on the ambiance, you could have fun and type up your menu for the occasion and print it for your guests (one menu could be shared by two, three people and randomly placed on the table) or you could write it up on a slate or blackboard for any casual ambiance like for the *Bistro* theme (chapter one). For the more formal menus, you could delicately hand-write each of them individually for your guests, provided you have nice penmanship. Menus are similar to handwritten, old-fashioned letters. They are rare and sweet and will add to the uniqueness and care of your dinner party.

CHAPTER 9

Ambiance Quintessentials

"The senses are the organs by which man places himself in connexion with exterior objects."
—Jean-Anthelme Brillat-Savarin

Aside from the visual and practical details that are involved in home entertaining, there are the indirect details that appeal to the five senses. These subtle tips are very important, perhaps more so than the food itself, as they set the mood for entertaining at home YOUR WAY. This is when you become the producer of your own show, giving a feel for who you really are to your friends, and conducted in a discreet and charming way. So, what are your props?

Lighting:

As any movie director knows, the lighting is the secret ingredient for creating an atmosphere. It is your way of setting the scene and its subtext by surrounding your guests with lights that deliver warmth and intimacy. Lighting is absolutely fundamental and not to be taken lightly—literally!

For any kind of entertaining, we recommend to keep the lighting at a low, subtle level in the living room, the dining room, the kitchen or wherever the dinner party is taking place. Plus, most people don't want to be flashed with too much light, as it tends to be unflattering for the complexion of you and your guest's skin.

As a rule of thumb, avoid switching on ceiling hard lights such as chandeliers or lanterns, but if you have to, then use them subtly. They can be on while your guests are enjoying a glass of Champagne, but not when you are ready to go sit at the table. Instead, favour table lamps throughout the room, and/or floor lights. If you have wall lights, halogen and spotlights, then make sure to dim them all. Actually, if you can avoid the halogen lamp all together, so much the better.

Music:

The proper musical choice is probably the most important of all the subtle tips. Music is one of the only art forms that can shape and change someone's mood from one second to the next. It can give you a huge sense of ease and pleasure or make you cry, or give you a migraine, all at the drop of a hat. That said, we stress that you only use relaxing or chill ambiance music. That doesn't mean sounds of whales in the ocean or a Buddhist mantra, but something universally liked by most people and where the conversations of your guests are not in competition with the music. This means no hard rock, metal, loud pop, or music that is too ethnic. We have listed specific playlists for all of our ambiances, to give you an idea. Generally speaking however, we recommend Bossa Nova, light rock, and jazz.

Scents and Candles:

Without overdoing it, you could add some scented candles, perfume sticks, incense, room diffusers, or a *"lampe de berger"* diffuser. Nothing too strong though. Avoid placing them in the dining area, as it will not mix well with the fine food you cooked up. We recommend adding some scents in your living room and guest bathroom.

This is a list of some scent suggestions by ambiance, from Part I of this book:

- *Bistro*: Havana, leather
- *Normandie:* Fresh cut grass, wood, verbena, lilac
- *Provence*: Lavender, fig, orange blossom
- *Marrakech*: Cinnamon, jasmine, tuberose, orange blossom, mint, patchouli
- *Mont Blanc*: Cedar, pine, musk, winter spice
- *Quai D'Orsay:* Leather, sandalwood, amber, musk
- *Mon Cheri: Pois de senteurs*, rose, lilac, lily of the valley, iris, violet
- *Rive Gauche:* Rose, pomegranate, grapefruit
- *Buffet La Petite Maison*: Lemongrass, lemon, wood
- *Buffet Le Louvre:* Vanilla, oak
- *Monte Carlo Grillade:* Mimosa, gardenia, sea air

- *Le Chasseur Grillade:* Musk, pine, wood
- *Aperitif Din-Din:* Amber, Sandalwood

Comfort:

There is a common misinterpretation around the French term *bien-vivre*, whereby it is associated with something expensive and high-end—and even snobby. This is not the case. *Bien-vivre* relates more to an idea of laid-back sophistication and casual elegance. It will already be conveyed by what we've covered: the food, the décor, the sensuous atmosphere and the soft lightning. However, it could not be complete without paying attention to many other comfort elements.The room where you will entertain needs to look comfortable but also needs to have a practical disposition.

What is important to check:

- If your chairs are a bit on the rigid side, don't hesitate to add some comfy cushions.
- The same thing goes for your sofa, where you can add a nice throw and decorative cushions.
- Make sure that your table is sturdy and not wobbly. It is a good idea to check it before and maybe add a little carton under a foot to balance the table out.
- Check the spacing between your chairs, allowing your guests sufficient elbow-room.

CHAPTER 10

The Food: It's Not Complicated

"Life is really simple, but we insist on making it complicated."
—Confucius

As the great Chinese philosopher suggests, let's keep life simple. The following easy recommendations will produce a superb effect on your guests whether you have an hour ahead of you or a week's time.

Pantry Essentials:

Whether for a last minute lunch or dinner with friends, or even planned occasions, there are some basic ingredients that you should almost always keep in your fridge and pantry. This is like a personal home entertaining kit. You just never know what may happen—a last minute added guest, or one or two ingredients that you forgot to buy while at the grocery store. Little surprises might pop up and it's best to be prepared. This goes for appetizers, main dishes and desserts. Here's what we suggest always having at home for those "you never know moments":

- Nuts: Almonds or cashews (for the *apéritif*).
- Meats: Sliced ham or prosciutto.
- Canned goods: Lentils or artichoke hearts, olives.
- Starch: Pasta or basmati rice.
- Dairy: Butter, eggs, cheese, plain yogurt (could be substituted for *crème fraiche* or sour cream).
- Frozen: Pie crust, shrimp, sea scallops, sorbets or ice cream (sorbets, of course, are better so you don't get tempted to eat ice-cream).
- Bread: Good quality sliced bread or various crackers.
- Staple Ingredients: Olive oil, vinegar, salt, pepper, some basic herbs (rosemary, *herbes de Provence*, thyme), lemons, parsley.
- Drinks: Still and sparkling bottled water, wine, fruit juices, and some basics for your bar rack (whiskey, vodka, gin, *crème de cassis*).

Basic Presentation Tips and Tricks:

It's all well and good to decide on a menu and to cook it, but if you don't pay a little attention to your presentation, then what you're serving will not have the same effect. Presentation is essential. It's like unwrapping a beautiful gift. Wouldn't you prefer to open a beautifully crafted gift than one with lousy paper and no bow or ribbon? The same applies here. The devil is in the details, and this is one big detail that is actually easy to achieve! We also strongly emphasize paying special attention to your presentation for the formal ambiances. We have selected four "gadgets" that will help you create a long lasting impression. Please note that these are not prescriptions, just suggestions.

Kitchen Essentials:

—The *Piquet.* Besides being a Medieval torture device, the other definition of it is an icing tip (a plastic bottle with a squeezing tip). Once you've poured any sauces, savory or sweet, into this instrument, you'll have fun by zig-zagging the gravy or the *coulis* around the plate. You can swirl the sauce or simply pour a small amount on the side.

—The *Cercle a Patisserie.* This is a baking ring. This utensil will help you transform your two or three types of ingredients into an elegant tower shape. You can purée some vegetables, place them in the ring, remove the mould, and voilà!

—The Rice Dome Trick: Rinse a shallow glass with cold water, dry it, and stuff the rice up to the top. Turn it upside down, like when you were a kid making sand castles on the beach. This gives you a beautiful dome shaped rice side dish.

—The Peeler: To obtain lacy strings of vegetables or fruits and to ornately decorate your plate here and there. Very easy to do with zucchini, oranges, lemon, and lime.

—Chinese Spoons: These are ideal to serve any type of *hors d'oeuvres* for the *apéritif.* Consider small scallops, duck mousse, and salmon eggs as a few examples.

Other Best Food Accessories:

Even if you buy a dessert or a vegetable dish almost already done, do not forget to add your own signature touch. This can be achieved by using one of the following ingredients:

—Parsley or Cilantro:

This is our personal favorite. Basically, for any savory dish, you can add parsley circled around dishes and then place one big parsley leaf centered in the middle of your dish. It doesn't get easier than this.

—Herbs:

You can use rosemary, thyme, bay laurel, chives, basil and lavender. For dessert, an excellent herb to put on your creation is a big mint leaf on top of your sorbet or chocolate mousse. The same idea goes with the spices, such as a stick of cinnamon or vanilla on top of a tagine or an apple tart.

—Mini Fruits and Vegetables:

These are also a sensational touch to make your dish more special. You can use cherry tomatoes, baby oranges (kumquats), grapes and red currents.

—Wine leaves:

These are perfect as a natural bed to welcome cheeses with walnuts or almonds.

Key Sauces:

Before we start with the types of meals, it is imperative that we share with you the three benchmark sauces for your salads, dishes and some vegetable accent dishes.

Dressing:

—*La vinaigrette:* This is made with a teaspoon of Dijon mustard, balsamic or white wine vinegar that you stir in and then slowly add the olive oil (in that order). You can also optionally add salt, pepper, *herbes de Provence*, and some pressed garlic. The vinaigrette will be suitable for all your salads and vegetable crudités. An alternative is also mustard, honey and oil dressing.

—Lemon-Garlic Dressing:

This is reserved for marinated fish, some green vegetables that you steam, broil or grill or also to pour on top of crudités salads. Simply press a couple of garlic cloves, add two lemons that are juiced together, add some olive oil, and finish with salt & pepper. Zesty!

—*La* Mayonnaise: For every mayo lover this is so easy to make. Start with a generous spoon of Dijon mustard, one egg yolk and mix. Then, slowly start pouring and stirring in the olive oil, until the mayonnaise is thick. You can also add a drop of chili sauce or *crème fraîche* as an extra tid-bit. Delicious!

Types of Meals:

Take some time to think about what type of meal you would like to make. The food should always be simple, light, tasty and well presented. That is the cornerstone to French cooking.

Once you know what type of meal you want to make, decide on how many courses you'd like to include. In order to reduce the stress, we emphasize that less is more. One of our favorites, if you are keen to invite at home often, is the "number three" formula: Appetizer + *Entrée* + Dessert

Widespread in most restaurants in France are three different meal formulas or *prix fixe* to choose from:

- Formula One: One main *entrée* or *plat du jour* (if pressed with time).
- Formula Two: One main *entrée*, plus either an appetizer or a dessert.
- Formula Three: Appetizer, main *entrée* and dessert, (you may also include cheese before the dessert).

You can apply all of our suggested thirteen ambiances to any of these three options.

Formula One:

Option one should only be chosen if you're in a rush or if you decide to organize a last-minute meal. Another appropriate setting is if you are planning to go to the theatre or opera and want to eat a little more than a nibble. Whatever it is, the food should be able to be made fast. Either you cook it the night before and heat it up last minute, or you can whip it up in less than twenty minutes. This is where the basic ingredients you have in your fridge and pantry come in handy. For this type of meal, the theme, by definition, is casual, so you can apply all the casual linens, plates, glasses and flatware you have available.

Formula Two:

The second option consists of one main *entrée* with its side dish, plus either an appetizer or a dessert. In this case, you should put the appetizer, main dish and side dishes on the table at the same time. Your guests can serve themselves in the order in which the dishes arrive, which can be subtly communicated by the host or hostess.

Formula Three:

Option three is more formal and follows classical French tradition. It requires more time to prepare and to eat. It also includes changing the plates in between each course (and even the wine too). The sequence is as follows:

- Appetizer
- *Entrée*
- Cheese
- Dessert
- Coffee or tea

In this complete menu option, which could be used for all of the casual as well as for all formal ambiances (except for the buffet ambiances), you will need to change your guests plates twice and their cutlery once. Having a trolley is handy in such a case.

Here's a tip: Avoid surprises! Always execute a dish that you are comfortable with. One time we made an *Hachis Parmentier* (a sort of French Shepherd's Pie), using the oven. But once it was cooked, it was impossible to detach it from its tin container. It was a real disaster that we hadn't thought about.

Types of Wine:

The types of wines listed below are broad suggestions. The kind of wine you choose will depend on the food you're serving—whether it is on the light or rich side, or whether your main course has fish or meat in it. Fortunately many of the regions in France offer all red, white and sometimes even rosé selections, however, try to avoid serving a white wine after a red wine, or a dry wine after a fruity wine. In sharing our suggestions for French wines, we've broken the wines by ambiance: formal and casual.

<u>Formal</u> (Mon Cheri, Rive Gauche, Le Quai d'Orsay ambiances)

- Burgundy: *Pommard, Vosne-Romanée, Puligny Montrachet*
- Bordeaux: *Chateau Margaux, St. Julien, Sauterne, St. Emilion*
- Beaujolais: *Fleurie, Chiroubles, Brouilly*
- Côtes du Rhone: *Chateauneuf du Pape, Gigondas, Vacqueyras*
- Champagne. You can serve Champagne for the *aperitif* or for the whole dinner, depending on your food and budget. However, please make sure it is from the *Champagne* region of France. Otherwise, it is considered a sparkling wine. Here—we will simply list the most available and widespread French Champagnes: *Moët-Chandon, Mumm, Piper Heidsieck, Veuve-Cliquot.*

<u>Casual</u> *(*Bistro, Normandie, Buffet, Grillades, Apéritif Din-Din ambiances)

- Southwest: *Cahors*
- Beaujolais: *Beaujolais Villages, Beaujolais Nouveau*
- Cotes du Rhone*: Vinsobre, Cairanne*
- Loire Valley: *Chinon, Bourgueil* (red wines from the *Touraine* region)

<u>Regional</u> (La *Provence,* Marrakech, *Mont Bl*anc ambiances*)*

- *La* Provence: *Coteaux d'Aix, Cotes du Ventoux, Cotes de Provence, Cotes du Rhone, Tavel,* and wines of Corsica (*Ajaccio* and *Patrimonio*).
- Marrakech: Wines from North Africa including the *Mascara* (from Algeria), or a *Boulaouane* (from Morocco).
- Mont Blanc: *Arbois (*from the Jura region), *Crepy* or *Apremont* (from the Savoie region).

CHAPTER 11

No More Stress. You Have A Game Plan!

People often worry about who to invite, how to seat them around, who is supposed to pour the wine, how to serve, and what should one think about and anticipate? Our suggestions will walk you through the entire process, just like a mini-rehearsal, and hopefully remove any logistical anxieties.

Who Does What?

If you're single, then depending on the type of ambiance you choose, and if you have the means, it is not a bad idea to hire one person to help you prepare and serve the food as well as to clean up. This is only for a formal setting or if you have more than eight guests. Otherwise, you can easily do it yourself. If you're hosting as a couple, then most of the work is shared (even though the woman traditionally does more, men are entertaining and cooking more and more these days). Regardless of whoever has the traditional "male" or "female" role, it is still important to clearly divide and conquer the work to avoid any confusion. The workload (for lack of a better word since you're supposed to have fun) depends on each person's tastes and competencies.

Person One:

One person will take the responsibility of cleaning the living room, dining room, guest bathroom and kitchen, adding flowers, rearranging some decoration pieces, finding candles, etc. This person also sets the table, cooks the food, serves the food, and if any guest bring flowers, places them in a vase and puts it in the living or dining area.

Whoever serves the guests will present the dish on the left side of the guest.

Person Two:

The second partner handles checking the lights and candles, helping with some of the cleaning, taking out the garbage and helping to prepare some of the food (like cutting onions, slicing the bread last minute, etc). The partner also makes sure that the bar is full. Once the guests arrive, he or she greets them, takes their coats, and offers them something to drink for the *apéritif.*

—The gender does apply while eating, as traditionally, the man is in charge of pouring the wine.

Wine is poured from the right side of the guest.

—Clearing the table of any empty dishes and used plates has to be negotiated beforehand.

Your Guests:

This brings us to your guest's role. Well, obviously, since you are inviting them to your home, you are there to offer your time, your food, and your drinks to them, and it is your pleasure to do so. Considering that your guests probably appreciate this kindness, (especially since we are rare in number these days to actually entertain at home), some of them may want to help you, and by all means, let them. They will feel like they are participating in the dinner party, which is a nice feeling to have. Do not be a martyr trying to do everything yourself as this is not the army. You and your guests came together to have a good time—don't forget that.

Who to Invite?

Now, this question should only be answered by the host and/or hostess. By and large, you should only invite people whose company you really enjoy. Don't invite people you kind of like because you feel obligated—unless, of course—you don't have the choice. That said, if you're inviting a mix of people, and some of them don't know each other, please keep these tips in mind:

- Plan ahead of time who you'd like to invite and how they can blend together. Some people are great at meeting other people, while others are not. Choose wisely. The point is for everyone to feel welcome, even for the more introverted, shy types.

- Pick an ambiance (like one of the thirteen we suggest in Part I of this book) and think of some topics of conversation you can use with your guests (just in case).
- Always invite at least one guest that is funny and can get along with nearly everybody. Someone who can warm up any room or situation, and has a good sense of humor is a great asset.
- Do not invite your guests via group email, where everyone is cc'd, or via social media. It is more personal if you invite everyone individually. If you don't have the time to invite them in person or on the phone, then just use the copy and paste tool and send your friends individual emails. By doing this, it makes them feel special and keeps the event a little mysterious. When you send an individualized email, give some idea as to what the guests can expect without saying too much. Here's an example:

Dear Ted,

In light of the amazing weather that the heavens have graced us with, I'm organizing a little summer din-din in my apartment. It will be a good occasion to see you and connect with some other friends I haven't seen in a while (even if we're all in the same city!). Anyway, we should be about 6 or 8 people, all cool folks, don't worry. If you want to bring a friend, just let me know two days before. Looking forward to seeing you soon. It will be at my place next Saturday, July 30th. Please let me know if you can make it.

—You (God or Goddess of Dinner Parties)

The Disposition of the Table

—Plates have to be of the same shape and color at all times as well as the glasses.

—Depending on which formula you opt for, the number of plates and cutlery varies as well as the glasses.

Formula One:

You just need one set of cutlery and two glasses (water and wine) plus one plate.

Formula Two:

You will adapt to your choice of having an appetizer and a main dish or a main dish and a dessert. Either way, you will need two plates. One must be small that you'll use for the appetizer or for the dessert, and one normal size plate for the main dish. One set of cutlery and two glasses (water and wine) will be perfect.

Formula Three:

You will use three plates. One normal size plate for dinner and two small ones for the appetizer and the dessert. Two glasses (water and wine) and two sets of cutlery are needed. If the ambiance is formal, you might need three glasses: a Champagne flute, next to the wine glass, and then the water glass on the far right.

The Countdown

There shouldn't be a military type of checklist—particularly if the event is casual and if you have a stocked fridge and pantry. However, a few tips to avoid worrying about at the last minute:

Two Days Before:

- Choose your menu.
- Buy your food and drinks.
- Make sure everyone has RSVP'd.
- Check that the oven works.

The Night Before:

- Clean your house.
- Organize the fridge so as to know what to find when you need it.
- Put away any clutter in the closets that the guests can see. You will notice that receiving guests over is a good kick in the butt for some of the chores you've been neglecting!

- Cook! Lots of our dish suggestions can be prepared the night before, like marinating a dish, cooking a *Boeuf Bourguignon*, boiling the artichokes or the asparagus or letting a chocolate mousse refrigerate overnight.
- Buy and arrange your flowers.
- Take out and check your linens. Are they all clean? Ironed? Have spots or stains?
- Double-check that you have enough plates, flatware, platters and glasses.
- Check that the bathroom is clean and stocked with toilet paper. Replace the hand soap with a new one, if necessary.
- Add any candles or scents you'd like.
- Choose what to wear for the occasion.
- Wash your hair either the night before or the morning of your event. You don't want to greet your guests with wet hair!

Late Afternoon or Early Evening on Party Day:

- In the kitchen, begin to prepare the cheese plate/tray, but be sure to cover it up.
  Note: some cheeses should be kept refrigerated until the last minute (goat cheese, brie, roquefort), so it is best to keep your cheese plate in the fridge until one hour before serving.
- Cook your food and check on its progress from time to time.
- Check that any drinks that need to be served cold are in the refrigerator like white wine, Champagne, sparkling water, and fruit juice.
- Check that your dessert is ready and nothing is missing (like any accompanying cookies, chocolates, etc.).
- Take a shower, get dressed and put on your make-up.
- Start playing some music, pour yourself a glass of wine and start getting into a good mood.

Thirty Minutes Prior to Party Time:

- Place the wine and water on the table.
- Put all the *hors d'oeuvres* for the *aperitif* out in the living area.
- Make sure you're ready with the drinks, ice and any napkins or bowls.

When Guests Arrive:

- Take their coats, offer them something to drink and stay with them.
- Introduce people to one another and relax.
- Then discreetly head for the kitchen and cut the bread. Take out the cold appetizers from the fridge and place them on the table.

Clothing Tips

Have you been wondering how to glam it up the French way?

For women:

As a rule of thumb, and in line with the psychological principles written in the second part of this book, it is best to find and keep your own style coherent with your attitude and personality. You should dress up for yourself in order to feel sexy, but without revealing too much. That would be a real *faux pas*!

Regardless of your size, from full-figured to petite, a Parisian woman's key articles of clothing revolve around an outfit that is not overdone and presents a clean silhouette with fluid lines. Style is about respecting your body shape while focusing on your subtle yet confident sex appeal. Through the shape and cut of garments, or with accessories like belts and cool jewellery, you can reveal a little, and all the while, remain mysterious and feminine. Do not hesitate to emphasize your waist, your shoulders or your cleavage.

Accessories are a must, and here again, it is about balance. Never wear big earrings with a big necklace at the same time, for instance. Don't match too much either like wearing the same color shirt and cardigan.

One accessory is usually not enough and it will be hidden in the rest of your outfit. It's best to compose different permutations such as: a necklace, bangle bracelets and a belt; or statement earrings and bangle bracelets; or tiny earrings and a long necklace like a *sautoir*. Remember that coordinating does not always equate to matching. It is about a nuanced equilibrium.

And the best is yet to come with the shoes—ahhhh, the shoes—the indispensable accessory which will glam up the whole look. High heels are a must, as they bring confidence and are the feminine attribute of excellence. High heels help shape the silhouette. There is no excuse for not wearing heals in your home, as you have very little walking to do (as oppose to walking to your office).

Your hair should of course be clean, and not too worked up, but more relaxed. In fact, let your hair down! The make-up should be natural, focusing more on your tint and health than on too much color. You can do this by applying a little powder and blush, and then adding mascara and a dash of lip-gloss.The whole idea is to stay subtle and sexy. If you want to apply more make-up that is fine too, but just remember to either focus the heavy colors on either the eyes or the lips—but not both together! For example, wearing bright red lipstick is sexy, but then tone it down on your eye make-up. The same is true vice versa. If you want to accentuate your eyes with dark shades of eye shadow and eyeliner, then use more natural, subtle tones for your lips. And of course, never forget to wear a little perfume!

For men:

For men's outfits, chill-chic works best. Wearing loafers, slacks, a nice shirt, and a jacket or suit, if it is a formal occasion will be lovely. Navy blue is always chic. Men can also wear nice jeans with a colorful shirt and a more traditional country jacket, adding a pocketed handkerchief that matches the color of the shirt. Here again, you don't need to dress to impress, but do put in some effort and most importantly, feel good about what you're wearing.

CHAPTER 12

They're Here

Ding-Dong!

The doorbell rings. Take a last minute mirror check. SMILE!

As soon as your guests arrive, don't forget the following: to *open the door with a smile!*

Don't appear tired or overwhelmed, but rise to this fantastic occasion. If people bring flowers, take them in the kitchen, put them in a vase and showcase them where the guests can see them. If your guests bring you wine, then only open it and use it for dinner if it blends with your meal. If people bring you chocolate or desserts, share it with them (don't keep it for yourself).

While you're introducing people for the first time, describe a little bit about who they are to one another. You don't have to feel like you're being put on the spot and must come up with an enormous amount of wit and humour. You can start by using the basics.This person is from so and so place, works at so and so and explain how you personally met them. If the people you're introducing to one another have something in common, then add that into your introduction. Never insult or intimidate people while you're first introducing them just because you're nervous.

L'Apéro

The *apéro*, which is a polite slang for *apéritif,* is the best part of the whole dinner party! It is the cocktail hour before the dinner. In our family, the *apéro* time is a religion. It is the best (and easiest) part of the dinner.

Since it marks the start of your dinner party, some of your guests are just tuning into the vibe of the ambiance, so they may appear a bit shy at first.

After all, they have left their comfort zones and arrived into your comfort zone. That is why it is so important to make them feel at ease right away. And, it is another big reason why you absolutely should not be panicking in the kitchen, but rather, catering to some delightful conversation with your guests. The mood of the entire evening starts with the *apéritif.* Pay particular attention to your more introverted guests, by talking with them yourself and complementing them.

The *apéro* is filled with light conversation, some jokes and getting to know each person better. With plenty of wine, Champagne and *hors d'oeuvres* going around the room, your guests begin to feel really at ease and are enticed by your kindness as well as by the ambiance's music, lighting and aromas.

Here's what you can serve for food and *apéro* drinks.

Typical *Apéro* Drinks:

- Champagne
- *Kir* (white wine with a dash of *crème de cassis* liquor)
- Whisky or Bourbon
- Sparkling water with a wedge of lemon or lime
- Fruit Juice (preferably fresh)

Typical Apéritif Hors D'oeuvres:

- Sliced *saucisson sec* or chorizo (preferably on a wooden board) or grilled *merguez* sausages (on a plate with toothpicks).
- Black and green olives.
- Carrots, fennel, cucumber, radishes, with hummus, guacamole or another kind of dip.
- Cashews, pistachios, almonds and whole peanuts (always fun).
- Rough cuts of Parmesan cheese.

Don't forget to also add small (but elegant) paper napkins and a few random bowls for your nutshells and other debris.

Diplomatic Seating Arrangements

Unless your dinner party is solely filled with really good, close friends, you should plan ahead where to seat your guests. Very close friends can be spontaneously seated, but if there is a mix of guests for a formal occasion, there are some nuanced ways to seat people so that everyone is satisfied. In France, there definitely is a hierarchical way of seating people.

In general, the host and hostess are seated at the head of the table—front and back. Placed on the right hand side of the host and hostess are any special guests (determined by age, social ranking, very old friend, etc.). The most special guest should be on the right hand side of the host/ hostess, and then on the left should be someone just as special but a little less important in age, social standing, etc. It is therefore a privilege to be seated next to the host and hostess.

Although it is sometimes difficult to have an equal amount of men and women, try to always keep the sequence of men and women side by side for the rest of the guests (as oppose to two women or two men sitting next to each other).

In France, we like to separate couples at the dining room table, in order to allow for interesting conversations with new people. In the same vein, if some friends are very close, do not sit them next to each other. They might spend the entire evening conversing by themselves and not mingle with the rest of the dinner party.

Aside from the seating based on hierarchy and the man-woman equilibrium rule, the most important, but subtle aspect of seating people is based on their personalities. Place people together who you think will enjoy each other's company. This is no place to test people. Let your guests have their fun.

And one last piece of advice: Avoid talking about politics or religion! But if you must, and it becomes a bit heated, you will have to diffuse it. The best way is to create a diversion by asking one of the guests who is in the middle of the argument to help you in the kitchen.

CHAPTER 13

Recommendations

The Art of Serving

The host and hostess are the first ones to start eating. The rest of the table follows suit. As the host, it might be a good idea to quickly explain the dishes being served. After all, you did take the time to buy, cook and present the food.

If you're serving a whole turkey, chicken, duck or the like, it is the host, or man, who cuts and serves the food around. If you're in a couple, the woman serves or passes around the side dishes. If you're hosting alone, then either cut up the main dishes in the kitchen right before, or let a volunteer or a male guest undertake this very masculine role. During formal occasions, it is better to serve your guests individually. However, there is no problem passing the dishes around the table for a more casual get together.

Always serve your guests in this order: Women first, then men (from oldest to youngest). The same sequence is applied for clearing out the table. Never pass empty dishes around, allotting one plate for all the leftover food and piling up the dishes. In France, that is considered very provincial or "red neck" to do.

The wine should be served by the host or man of the house. If you're single, then you could serve the wine yourself, or just like with cutting up the meat, delegate it to a nice male guest at the table. If the wine is from a good year, announce it and have a few guests taste test it before serving it to the other guests.

After the cheese is served, clear the table of everything (salt, pepper, mustard, vinaigrette, bread, etc). Then bring the dessert on the table with the dessert plates and flatware. If you're serving pie or cake, cut it and serve it directly on the table in front of your guests. Do not cut it in the kitchen as it will ruin the shape and décor of the dessert.

When the host or hostess feel like the time spent at the dining room table is coming to an end, it is up to him or her to invite all the guests to the living room for coffee or herbal tea, or a *digestive* (which is an after dinner drink that is usually quite strong like a cognac, brandy, or grappa). If you choose to serve digestives, please be sure to have the proper glasses. You absolutely cannot serve a cognac in a wine glass.

Children

During the week, small children are in bed by the time your guests arrive. On weekends however, they can be included during the *Apéritif,* but have to say goodnight when it is time to go to the dinner table. It will allow the hosts to be more attentive to their guests. If they are teenagers, chances are they are not going to want to be with the adults anyway!

If your guests ask you whether they can bring their child or children, try to make a little children's table near the dining area if possible. The children's menu should be the same as the adult meal, albeit a little smaller in portions, and of course, no alcohol! The *Buffet* ambiance is fantastic for including children.

Guest Etiquette

- Bring a gift to your host such as flowers, candles, wine, chocolates, macaroons or anything that you know they will enjoy.
- Do not bring along your pet unless you have checked with the host.
- RSVP as quickly as you can whether you can attend or not.
- Do not stay too late. Usually guests stay on because they do not want to be the first one to leave!

ABOUT THE AUTHORS

Anne de Montarlot

Anne graduated with a distinction in 2003 from Sheffield University (UK) with an M.A in counseling. She wrote a thesis on *Connectedness*, believing that therapy is one of the best ways of improving one's sense of connection and can easily transform the experience of living. Aside from her practice in London (www.re-solutionpartnership), her other passion has been around food and conviviality.

Anne was born in France, lived in New York, where she worked in finance and advertising, lived in Monaco and is now living and working as a psychotherapist and Life Coach in London. During her 25 years of expatriate experience, entertaining at home represented an anchor and has always been, for her, the best way of connecting with people.

Bahia de Montarlot

Born in Paris, and raised in New York, Bahia de Montarlot is a Franco-American entrepreneur and contemporary furniture designer for her brand, Bahia Style (www.BahiaStyle.com).

She currently resides in Manhattan, N.Y. Prior to launching her own brand, Bahia worked in home decor for a decade for large retail stores in France and the United States. She graduated from Fordham University, and while a student, worked for the International Herald Tribune in Paris, France, as well as the United Nations in New York.

Bahia has published articles for the New York Times and enjoys climbing mountains. She has successfully made the summit of Mt. Rainier (Washington, US) and Mt. Kilimanjaro (Tanzania).

After hosting countless memorable dinner parties in New York, Bahia's friends pressured her and her sister to write a book that would share their unique knowledge. Hence the two sisters got down to the "nitty gritty" to co-author their first book, *Host With Confidence: The French Secrets.*